Twayne's United States Authors Series

Sylvia E. Bowman, *Editor*

INDIANA UNIVERSITY

Conrad Aiken

CONRAD AIKEN

---

by FREDERICK J. HOFFMAN
University of California, Riverside

TUSAS 17

Twayne Publishers, Inc.   ::   New York

To E. C. and C. E.

Preface

CONRAD AIKEN is one of the most remarkable figures modern American literature has produced. The extent and variety of his writings are so impressive as to defy classification, or so it may seem at the beginning. But, within the richness of conception and the quantity of result, some essential themes persist; and they are developmental—that is, they grow in clarity and importance as Aiken's many approaches to them gradually diminish and as Aiken's grasp of the fundamental distinctions between major and lesser forms becomes more certain. Ultimately, the product is impressive, not for its quantity and variety but for its excellence and depth.

I have undertaken this study of Conrad Aiken for several reasons. For one, it has always seemed to me that he is a neglected figure in American literature: partly, because his own contemporaries (he is of the generation of T. S. Eliot and Ezra Pound) jumped into a position of prominence from which it was impossible to dislodge them; partly, because he has refused to yield to the temptation to become fashionable (he is one of the most acute critics of literature, including his own, in modern letters); finally, because his best work required the kind of close critical reading that was rarely practiced in the time when it appeared (1931-1936). It is to his lasting credit that R. P. Blackmur saw the value of Aiken's poetry in its own time; he was almost the only one who did so. Oddly, Aiken's reputation was slow in growing despite the fact that he was one of the first modern American poets to receive a full-length study; and Houston Peterson's *The Melody of Chaos* (1931) was written before Aiken's best work had appeared.

But my decision to study Aiken is not simply a matter of redressing balances. The development of Aiken's mind is intrinsically valuable. It is also a fascinating story, involving personal experience (which Aiken has brilliantly defined for us in *Ushant*), the writer as critic, and the slow growth of a precision of thought and its transference to art. He is a "representative" mind; in a limited sense, he is a "cultural hero" who takes it upon himself to articulate a special, personal *Weltan-sicht*. No one has so exhaustively and so elaborately explored the problems of the modern consciousness. That story is itself a sufficient reason for giving him the kind of attention that preparing for a book of this sort requires.

In Chapter I, I have tried to express the initial problem of consciousness, drawing from *Ushant* but especially from Aiken's many appearances as a critic over a period of four decades or so. Chapter II tries to define the special circumstances of the "fictional ego," as manifested in the short stories and novels. The final four chapters are concerned with the poetry—not only because Aiken's poetry represents almost three-fourths of the total product, but because it is as a poet that Aiken must finally be judged. Chapter III is devoted to his beginnings as poet; Chapter IV, to the special method of the "Symphonies" and its results; Chapter V, to the great work of his maturity, the Preludes of 1931 and 1936; Chapter VI, to the other works of the 1930's and beyond. It will, I hope, be seen that Aiken, as he develops, writes with a surer eye and ear, with a greater sense of limit and control, and with an ability to keep the more extravagant ranges of his talent in useful check.

This book is a "reading" of Aiken's work. It does not pretend to be definitive, but I do believe it will serve as a genuinely useful and worth-while introduction to the work of an exciting American man of letters.

FREDERICK J. HOFFMAN

The University of California
Riverside
August, 1961

Contents

Chronology

1889   August 5, birth of Conrad (Potter) Aiken, Savannah, Georgia. His parents were transplanted New Englanders: father, a physician and surgeon; mother, daughter of William James Potter, minister of First Congregational Society at New Bedford, Massachusetts, for much of his career. (See "Note" to *Skylight One*.)

1900   Aiken (eleven and one-half years old) discovers both
or   father and mother dead after murder-suicide. Aiken's two
1901   brothers adopted by a family in Philadelphia; Conrad went to live with a great, great aunt in New Bedford, Massachusetts, thus "claiming" the New England cultural inheritance of his family.

1907   Entered Harvard University, class of 1911, having been graduated from the Middlesex School, Concord.

1910-   President of Harvard *Advocate* to which, and to the
1911   Harvard *Monthly*, he made many contributions.

1911   In his senior year at Harvard, placed on probation for irregularity in class attendance. In protest, left Harvard and went to Europe for about six months (first of many trips to Europe): winter in Italy, Switzerland, France. Returned to Harvard to finish work on undergraduate degree.

1912   June, received Harvard degree; married a few days later, honeymoon in Italy, France, and England. Began writing poems for first published volume.

1914   *Earth Triumphant*, poems, first of forty-two volumes of verse, fiction, and criticism to appear in his career. (See bibliography for full list.)

1915   Moved with his family from Cambridge to Boston "in order to be near [John Gould] Fletcher who had recently returned from England." (Houston Peterson, *The Melody of Chaos*, p. 43.)

1916-1922   Several trips abroad; became acquainted with Ezra Pound, T. S. Eliot, Amy Lowell, and other poets and critics in England and in Massachusetts. Began career as critic and reviewer (chiefly of contemporary poets) for American magazines (*New Republic, Poetry Journal, Dial* [of which he was a contributing editor, 1917-1918], the Chicago *Daily News, Poetry,* and others). Wrote "Letters from America" to the London *Athenaeum* and London *Mercury.* Creative work mostly in poetry, of which several volumes published in these years.

1922   Winter, settled in England with his family: a few months in London, then (spring of 1923) to Winchelsea, a village in East Sussex, in south of England.

1924-1925   Winter, moved to Rye, east Sussex.

1925-1926   Returned to America; brief trip to Spain, summer of 1926.

1927-1928   Tutor in English, Harvard University.

1930   Received Pulitzer Prize for *Selected Poems* (published late 1929); also The Shelley Memorial Award.

1934   Received Guggenheim Fellowship. Began "London Letters" to the *New Yorker* (to 1936), under pseudonym of Samuel Jeake, Jr.

1937   Contributed essay on "Literature" to Federal Writers' Project Guide to Massachusetts: *Massachusetts: A Guide to Its Places and People.*

1945   Edited *Twentieth Century American Poetry.*

1946   Play, based on short story "Mr. Arcularis" (in *Among the Lost People,* 1934) accepted for production by The Company of Four, London, with Diana Hamilton working on the adaptation, Aiken assisting. As *Fear No More,* it played in London for four weeks in August and September.

1950-1951   Served in Library of Congress, Chair of Poetry (one of two one-year terms).

1951   *Mr. Arcularis,* play based on short story of that name, revised from London production, *Fear No More,* produced in "Arena Theatre," Washington, D. C.

1952   Conrad Aiken number of *Wake* magazine (New York City), with original and reprinted work by Aiken, Malcolm Cowley, Malcolm Lowry, others: an important event in reassessment of Aiken's work.

1953   *Collected Poems* won National Book Award as the most distinguished volume of poems published that year.

1958   Received The Gold Medal in Poetry from the American Academy of Arts and Letters.

Conrad Aiken

CHAPTER 1

Introduction:
The Trial of Consciousness

I

CONRAD AIKEN presents in *Ushant* his own record of an event of crucial importance. Not only the event but its impact on the observer was significant. In Savannah, Georgia, where he had been born in 1889, an eleven-year-old boy discovered both parents dead after an act of murder and suicide.

> . . . He was retaining all this, and re-enacting it, even to the final scene of all: when, after the desultory early-morning quarrel, came the half-stifled scream, and then the sound of his father's voice counting three, and the two loud pistol-shots; and he had tiptoed into the dark room, where the two bodies lay motionless, and apart, and, finding them dead, *found himself possessed of them forever.*[1]

No one can do more than speculate upon the full impact of this experience. In addition to the horror of it, there was the fact of its having meant the end of one way of life and the beginning of another, totally different. The family dispersed, two of Aiken's brothers going to Philadelphia and Conrad himself to New Bedford, Massachusetts, a sea town fifty miles south of Boston.[2] In *Ushant,* Aiken refers to the event as establishing the course of his life and of his writing. He was always, so he says, in the act of "going back," of trying to regain that room, that house, in Savannah. Hadn't his entire life been simply a locus, he asks in *Ushant* (300), "bending itself again and again, after no matter how many interruptions and diversions, as of wars, or storms at sea, to this limit, this perhaps unattainable limit, this imperishable Ushant?"

The book *Ushant* is in itself a marvel of revelation. Aiken calls it "an essay"; and it is not an autobiography in any conventional sense. Instead, it is a record of his "stream-of-consciousness" memory, in some ways not unlike parts of the 1927 novel, *Blue Voyage*. But in *Ushant* a mature Conrad Aiken, grown out of all experimental hesitations about his career, speculates brilliantly about the past, using the major image of the "great circle": of the man circling back upon his youth, of being forced to swerve from it by the horror of its climax, and of beginning once again the encircling passage.

Both Savannah and New Bedford are sea towns; and the sea plays an intimately significant role in Aiken's literary maneuvers. There are the two images of the voyage (ostensibly an attempt at recovery, actually a move toward personal revelation and confession), and the central inhibition. This latter is symbolized in the title of Aiken's autobiographical essay: *Ushant* is obviously a pun, how much and how elaborate a pun we can appreciate only after thoroughly comprehending the record of which it serves as title. It is an Anglicization of the name Île d'Ouessant, an island off the Breton coast, which, dangerous to ships, warns them away from its channels and its approaches. Aiken's voyages to Europe—to England, mainly—are conceived in *Ushant* as being the principal adventures in the "great circle" experiences.

On one voyage, he tells us, he had been gradually awakening from a dream when he heard the alarm signals of his boat as it turned north from the dangerous shoals near the Île d'Ouessant. The dream was involved with one of his childhood experiences: ". . . They were reading a book, they were about to resume reading a book, four people sitting down in a nursery schoolroom to translate a book from the German," when the alarm bells sounded; so the question of the translation and the signal of alarm were confused: ". . . The four reader-participators all with the same name were now locked in endless and complex discussion as to *what it all meant*" (*Ushant*, 29-30).

To put it simply, perhaps bluntly and crudely, Conrad Aiken had in 1900 begun a voyage—a series of voyages that symbolically realized themselves as variants of one—on the surface of the earth in an effort to recapture a stability ("The finished forms and rituals of a fixed and conscious society") of which he had suddenly and terribly been deprived (*Ushant*, 303). It was as much a voyage of the consciousness as of the body—or, more so, a variety of adventures of the sensibility and mind, an effort to live "as richly, and beautifully, as possible, . . ." as his parents had done before their abrupt and unexpected and violent end (*Ushant,* 303).

Partly, the measure of the experience can be found in its recurrences in Aiken's art. Using this limited resource, we may point out the several varieties of compulsion and guilt which motivate the characters of many short stories and one or two of the novels. Both the title and the principal section of the novel *Great Circle* (1933) testify to its importance. In general, the struggles of Aiken's heroes to establish an emotional middle ground—between an extreme hatred of the flesh, of the corruptibility of the human species, and an emotional void—seem to be in one way or another efforts to recover a lost balance and stability from the past. Many of the short stories are centrally concerned with this kind of tension: the illusion of a gracious and sophisticated society, and the insistent threat posed by a naturalistic reduction (or annihilation) of its pretenses. The aesthetic virtue in Conrad Aiken's work is always menaced by the chaos from which it has been rescued. Throughout, the conflict of form and violence recurs in a hundred manifestations.

II

Most important, Aiken's writings—perhaps all of them—are essentially an attempt to recover consciousness, to re-establish it on a secular basis. This effort comprehends several patterns in the work itself: the preoccupation with the artist as person; the uncomfortable sense of separation, of isolation, from "raw life," which leads both to a contempt of it and a sense of "inferiority" to it; the constant search for a "compromise" with the flesh, manifested in the frequent experiments in adultery in which his characters are engaged; the compulsion to suffer and to offer oneself as a secular Christ in an anxiety-burdened crucifixion; the fearsome and fearful preoccupation with death, and —on another level—with the nihilation of consciousness.

In *Ushant,* again, Aiken speaks of his concern "with the evolution of consciousness . . . as being, for *homo sapiens,* or *homo incipiens,* the only true teleological 'order of the day,' his share in the great becoming fiat in the poietic of the great poem of life, his share—if one preferred to call it so—in the self-shaping of Godhead, or the only thing we knew it by, the mind of man" (*Ushant,* 175). The only religion that was any longer "tenable or viable," he maintained, was "a poetic comprehension of man's position in the universe, and of his potentialities as a poietic shaper of his own destiny, through self-knowledge and love" (*Ushant,* 220).

Aiken's writings are perhaps the most thoroughgoing effort in modern literature to establish a formal and a secular refuge from the threat of chaos. More than that, they are dominated by a formal dialectic, comprehending the relationship of consciousness and form to the universe. Superficially, the poles of this dialectic are living and dead matter; the human consciousness mediates between the two, dramatically rescuing living forms from death and insistently risking its own obliteration in the process.

Joseph Warren Beach correctly defines this matter as a "moral terror." It is abundantly clear, he says in *Obsessive Images* (1960), "that the revulsion recorded by Aiken is not, as in other poets, against the evil in men's hearts, their viciousness; that the sense of guilt does not enter into this feeling; and that there is not the faintest hint of what would ordinarily be considered theological implications. . . ."[3] The terror is related to the shock of Conrad Aiken's discovery in 1900; but it would be a mistake to assume that he remained fixed in a state of moral paralysis. Rather, following Beach's description of the process, we may say that the initial terror freed him from (or forced him to break from) conventional moral resources and initiated a lifelong search for balances and formal securities that had neither theological nor institutional supports. The key word is *consciousness,* by which he means the refinement of consciousness, a tenacity of purpose in maintaining and elevating it. As he wrote in a letter to me in 1944, the only "philosophic order" he finds necessary consists of "a belief in the evolution of consciousness, awareness, as our prime gift and obligation, and a Socratic desire to get on with it at all costs."[4]

There are many indications of this interest. At times it seems to take the simple form of delight in a heightened consciousness; as when he praises D. H. Lawrence's "terrific endowment of 'consciousness.'"

If we like, we can see his whole literary career as one prolonged and desperate and exhausting effort to be as conscious as possible. Everywhere, in his work, we encounter a burning fever of awareness; everywhere, we find ourselves involved in the same bloodshot tissue, a tissue positively vascular, so heavy is the raw network of veins and nerves. . . .[5]

But the delight is never free of qualification; for the consciousness in which Aiken puts his trust is a heightened, refined, sophisticated state of mind; an "aesthetic" awareness, as distinguished from a mere grasping for experience. It is very much akin to what Santayana calls the "realm of spirit," or sensations, passions, the pressure of the mind upon matter, with the object of "elevating" and shaping it.[6] More characteristically, Aiken speaks (*Freeman,* June 21, 1922) of Katherine Mansfield's "pure genius," of her "characteristic intensity—a kind of white heat of sensibility and awareness . . ." (ABC, 297). That is, while intensity and awareness are powers in themselves, they must have a formal and—by implication in Aiken's own use of them—a social context.

This is not to accuse Aiken of snobbery, or to suggest that he will accept "refinement" at the expense of power of will. He is primarily concerned to give the human consciousness as civilized and as strong a formal place as art can provide for it. But it is to be a secular, existentialist context; it is to be endured without the fashionable or traditional securities against a frank acceptance of it.

In *Ushant* he speaks of the great wonder and admiration he felt for the early work of T. S. Eliot, and especially for the doctoral study of the philosophy of F. H. Bradley which Eliot had written at Harvard; then he regrets that Eliot had shifted his ground in later years—from despair, Aiken says, of "the apparent chaos which blazed and swarmed and roared beyond the neat walls of Eden . . ." (*Ushant,* 215). And, reviewing Eliot's *For Lancelot Andrewes* (*Dial,* July, 1929), Aiken again regrets the fact that "Mr. Eliot seems to be definitely and defeatedly in retreat from the present and all that it implies" (ABC, 185).

Perhaps the most crudely simple statement of Aiken's belief— and of the problems it suggests—is in the sketch called "Gehenna" (in *Among the Lost People,* 1934). Not a story, but merely a monologue or reflection, it is actually a restatement of ideas developed in one phase of the novel *Blue Voyage* (1927). The Smith, or Jones, or Robinson, who is his "narrator," speaks of his relationship to the "great world," which can so easily "go to pieces." In its simple form, this reflection puts the case for human consciousness starkly and even with a melodramatic sense of finality. What, he asks, are these walls, this floor, these objects I see?

> Arrangements of atoms? If so, then they are all perpetually in motion; the whole appearance is in reality a chaotic flux, a whirlwind of opposing forces; they and I are in one preposterous stream together, borne helplessly to an unknown destiny. I am myself perhaps only a momentary sparkle on the swift surface of this preposterous stream. My awareness is only an accident; and moreover my awareness is less truly myself than this stream which supports me, and out of which my sparkle of conscious-ness has for a moment been cast up. . . .[7]

This kind of characterless, monologic inbreeding is a typical example of "romantic naturalism," of which there were in litera-ture and art many other demonstrations, headed by (and often inspired by) Bertrand Russell's "A Free Man's Worship" (1918). The problem in Aiken's career was not how to state the situation, but how effectively to define and to dramatize it. To the tasks of definition and dramatization, Aiken addressed himself again and again. He never achieves absolute definition, but he makes a poetry out of approaches to, or "preludes to," definition.

As R. P. Blackmur has so aptly stated, a "prelude" in Conrad Aiken's poetry is "a beginning or approach, the taking up of a theme or the search for a theme, a promise, but not, finally, the thing itself except by implication."[8] That is, the reality for Aiken is not the situation described in "Gehenna" so much as it is the movement toward and away from it, the state of mind at the moment of its experience of universalizing a condition, of being aware of it. This central problem involves the description of both the "reality principle" itself and the psychic condition of the conscious person. If we add the *social* context of the experience, we may comprehend all of Aiken's attempts to create literature from this central circumstance. With varying degrees of success and failure, his short stories, novels, poetry, and criticism are concerned with it.

III

Among other things, Conrad Aiken was a journeyman reviewer. He undertook reviewing not only as a means of livelihood but also—in the manner of several of his contemporaries—as a way of responding to the work of others and to the experience of reading it. The result is an amazing record of good taste and good judgment. I can think of no twentieth-century critic with so good a record of "hits" and "near misses." His aim was not invariably true, but it was so often at or near the target as to make the exceptions rare indeed. He was, therefore, an uncommonly good judge of contemporary literature, and he maneuvered skillfully between the extremes of experiment and traditionalism. Until 1958, only the early volume *Scepticisms* (1919) existed as testimony of his value; in the later year, the excellent editing by Rufus Blanshard of one hundred and two of Aiken's more than two hundred occasional pieces firmly established his critical reputation.

Both volumes[9] are invaluable for a number of reasons. They offer one man's history of modern letters; they are in themselves a history of the changes in his critical vocabulary; and they support our reflections about his principal theoretical judgment. As for the first of these, Aiken was from the beginning involved in and aware of the values of the "new Movements" in literature. He was able to speak of their excesses and of their genuine qualities without fear or favor. He did not spare himself: three of the pieces in *ABC* are about himself and prove his powers of self-criticism. He had his strong prejudices: there is little good to say of Ezra Pound (the "Rabbi Ben Ezra" of *Ushant*); and the Eliot of *For Lancelot Andrewes, Ash-Wednesday,* and after seems unfortunately to have retreated from the twentieth century. Among his preferences, Maxwell Bodenheim seems an unhappy choice; but it is interesting to see that of the many references to him in *Scepticisms*, none remains in *ABC*, a book which Aiken himself said "represents what I wish to preserve of the work done in those forty-odd years" (ABC, 10).

A sampling of the two volumes demonstrates the sharpness of Aiken's critical mind. It should also be pointed out that each of the essays is a "set piece," carefully arranged and thought out; Marianne Moore, who engaged him frequently for reviews in the *Dial,* spoke of him as "the perfect reviewer, Diogenes' one honest man, fearing only to displease himself. . . ."[10]

Of the "new poetry" he said in 1917 that "The bizarre has frequently been mistaken for the subtle; . . . The Imagists, straying too far in search of flowers of vividness and colour, have ended by losing themselves in a Plutonian darkness of unrelated sensory phenomena. . . ."[11] The "intellectual equipment" of Edgar Lee Masters has "about it . . . something of the *nouveau riche* . . ." (*Scepticisms,* 72). When Aiken is tempted wholly to admire, and to emulate, the work of another poet, he almost always pulls back from it to give it a second look for the flaws that may be not only in it but in his admiration of it. This is true of his judgment of the poetry of John Gould Fletcher, which at one time immensely attracted him. It is, he said finally, "a sort of absolute poetry, a poetry of detached waver and brilliance, a beautiful flowering of language alone, a parthenogenesis, as if language were fertilized by itself rather than by thought and feeling . . ." (*Scepticisms,* 112).

Aiken is especially perceptive in his several essays on Eliot. His study of *The Waste Land* (*New Republic,* February 7, 1923) was the shrewdest of its time. That great poem, he said, is not "in any formal sense, coherent," but is rather a "series of sharp, discrete, slightly related perceptions and feelings, dramatically and lyrically presented, and violently juxtaposed . . ." (ABC, 180). Of Eliot's later work, however, only *Murder in the Cathedral* seemed to him to have "the quality of greatness"; it suggested that Eliot had become "human and tender, with a tenderness and humanity which have nowhere else in our time found such beauty of form" (*New Yorker,* July 13, 1935; ABC, 192).

Among his predecessors, Aiken paid special attention to Emily Dickinson and Henry James. Of Miss Dickinson's manner, he spoke admiringly: "Once adjust oneself to the spinsterly angularity of the mode, its lack of eloquence or rhetorical speed, its naïve and often prosaic directness, one discovers felicities of thought and phrase on every page. The magic is terse and sure . . ." (*Dial,* April, 1924; ABC, 162).[12]

Concerning James, his judgment was more sharply qualified. In his famous *Criterion* review of April, 1925, he wrote of James and Whitman as "at opposite ends of a given spectrum." What Whitman loved in America "was exactly what [James] himself saw and fled from." And he concluded his study of the two American giants by saying that "James was the *subtler* critic, in the sense that he was immensely more perceptive and finely analytic of the communicative aspects of art; but Whitman was the wiser. He was a shrewd, though slipshod, judge of literature's psychological values in art, seeing more clearly the functional position of art in the human scheme. . ." (ABC, 231, 233).

But Aiken's criticism is valuable beyond the pleasure in sampling its insights. It is interesting to watch the growth of his critical mind, which improves as his status as a creative artist matures. He is at first much interested in "colour," and uses the term honorifically in many early reviews; we may assume he means by it both quantity and liveliness of poetic vocabulary, as well as the skill in communicating rhythmic patterns. He is drawn to what he calls the "absolute poetry" of John Gould Fletcher's "Symphonies," though he also detects the flaws. He shies away from conventional tributes to religious iconographies and is inclined to admire poets who hold "creeds and schools in abeyance."

In his early years as a poet, Aiken tries to find in contemporary poets and pundits support for his own position, one not fully or well defined. While he is intuitively "right" again and again in measuring his contemporaries, the reasons for his choices are more interesting perhaps than the fact that they are choices. He dislikes triviality[13] and mere cleverness; he seeks a style that he describes as "psycho-realistic"; he does not object to luxuriance of style, but he also sees the dangers of mere indulgence in "style" without intellectual substance.

Aiken's criticism from the beginning had a basis in a theory of "inspiration" which made distinctions among types of sensibility. For him, craftsmanship was "style," and "style" often (perhaps too often) meant richness, a lavish endowment of vocabulary and rhythms. This approach to poetry was indispensably equivalent to his view of the role of consciousness in the modern secular religion. Basic to his conception of art was the idea of subconscious resources; he speaks of the "subconscious treasure" of the artist, which is a treasure precisely because it is nourished by an uncommon sensibility: ". . . in the case of the poet who is, however intermittently, a genuine poet, one may safely say, I think, that it is when he is most the craftsman that he is least magically the poet. Craftsmanship is the skill with which the poet turns his subconscious treasure to account . . ." ("Magic or Legerdemain?" 1919; ABC, 45).

It would be a harmful distortion to speak of Aiken's criticism as exclusively "Freudian." Freud was important to him, but he could scarcely have offered him all he needed. In the words of Henry A. Murray, psychoanalyst and friend, Aiken was almost alone among the moderns who "allowed the Freudian dragon to swallow him, and then, after a sufficient sojourn in its maw, cut his way out to a new freedom. When he emerged he was stocked with the lore of psychoanalysis, but neither subjugated nor impeded by it. . . ."[14] The role of Freudian psychoanalysis is important, however far Aiken reached beyond it. In an early critical essay (*New Republic*, April 11, 1923), he deplores the vagueness and the unsystematic nature of most "aesthetic criticism," and he proceeds to the functional question of the role of art in the life of civilized man: ". . . there can be no *fundamental* distinction between the sense of beauty as afforded by the content and the sense of beauty as afforded by the form: both are alike, in essence, the satisfaction due to a successful wish-fulfilment; and both, in the ideal work of art, are present . . ." (ABC, 63).

That is, there is a deep hunger for "fulfillment" in the artist, a drive toward formal expression and toward the endowment of his craft. Speaking in the *North American Review* (December, 1917), of a book by Nicolas Kostyleff, *Le Mécanisme cérébrale de la pensée*, Aiken comes to this semi-Freudian conclusion about inspiration: "It is to some deep hunger, whether erotic or not, or to some analogous compulsion, that we must look for the source of the power that sets in motion the delicate mechanism on another plane, which M. Kostyleff has begun to illuminate for us . . ." (ABC, 41).

If we may come back once more to the question of "consciousness," as Aiken has frequently raised it, we can speculate upon two complementary forces that, in his theory of art, exist in tension. There is the pressure within, driving outward toward formal expression, toward "fulfillment" (in a much more narrow sense, this is Freud's "pleasure principle"). Pushing against it is the force from without, the shock of reality, which continually challenges the creative spirit and, in moments of terror or violence, may even severely dislocate it. These two forces reach a balance—more accurately, a tension—in the work of art, which is the highest and the most important of secular expressions.

Ultimately, this theory departs radically from the limitations of Freud's speculative considerations of art. The two pressures, as Aiken sees them, are both equally formal and formless. It is not simply a question of the forms (which exist beyond the id) being imposed upon the instinctual drives; instead, both the subconscious and the forces in reality invite formalization. In its final sense, Aiken's criticism (and much of his poetry as well) is a dialectical maneuvering of the two forces, but one without finality or synthesis. Language and rhythm are used to meet (to match) the energy of these external forces; there is a continual thematic exchange between chaos and language.

The word is identified with a move toward (a "prelude to") definition; but this definition dissolves, or partially dissolves, and leads to a new exercise of the imagination. It is a continuing process of intellectual and emotional motion forward and of withdrawal. As a result, the language often suffers an obfuscating richness (like the ink of the squid, defensively emitted); also, the relationship, as Aiken sees it, is never static (nor even stabilized), but always in flux, reaching for but never achieving definition.

That this theory of literature is related to the "moral terror" of which Professor Beach has spoken, and to the actual physical terror of Aiken's childhood experience, I think the evidence of *Ushant* will testify throughout his career. Aiken's work shows alternately a despair of life (and a wish to hide from it in art) and the desire to demonstrate a vigorous "aesthetic heroism" in meeting its challenge. The rhythms of these interchanges (which we might call "thematic dialectics" were it not for the ugliness of the phrase) are "unusual" in the broadest sense. They are called so in another of Aiken's essays, "Counterpoint and Implication" (*Poetry*, June, 1919), written in explanation of his "symphonies," his first major poems: "Granted that one has chosen a theme—or been chosen by a theme!—which will permit rapid changes of tone, which will not insist on a tone too static, it will be seen that there is no limit to the variety of effects obtainable . . ." (ABC, 128).

Of course, there *is* a limit to the possibilities, as Aiken himself later acknowledged. Aiken's view of the "symphony" involved the manipulation of what he called "emotion-masses," by which we assume he meant tonal qualities of rhythm and language. The qualitative difference between the "Symphonies" of the early years and the "Preludes" of the 1930's is essentially a substantive difference. The early poetry is charged with "colour," in the manner of Fletcher's rhythmical use of greens and greys, but it is relatively lacking in substance.

Not that Aiken failed to provide a variety of themes in the "Symphonies"; they not only are thematic, but are dramatically developed. It is only when he addressed himself to metaphysical definition and exploration that he lowered the intensities and the obvious richness of his effects. It is in this latter phase (*Preludes for Memnon*, 1931; *Time in the Rock*, 1936) that he becomes truly the "metaphysical poet"; and the substance of his observations relies much more stringently upon the poetry than does that of the early work.[15]

The essay "Counterpoint and Implication" nevertheless contains much that illuminates Aiken's critical—and, by implication, his philosophical—position. He suggests in it a technical obligation of the artist to communicate themes and ideas through nuances and tones. It may be that the result is too often a succession or a pattern of tones, with too little regard for meaning, or with one too obvious and too little explored to be significant. Frequently in his poetry before 1925, Aiken displays a virtuosity, an incredible range of tone and rhythmic skill, but the intellectual substance is slight and repetitious; or Aiken is given to relying upon assertion to carry him from one burst of tonal effects to another.

> Not content to present emotions or things or sensations for their own sakes—as is the case with most poetry—this method takes only the most delicately evocative aspects of them, makes of them a keyboard, and plays upon them a music of which the chief characteristic is its elusiveness, its fleetingness, and its richness in the shimmering overtones of hint and suggestion. Such a poetry, in other words, will not so much present an idea as use its resonance . . . (ABC, 129).

[28]

This is obviously to take too much away from the poetry to give to the music. It is a form of *symbolisme,* though it goes beyond the implicative strategies of that school. We may also say that it is a theory (and leads to a poetry) that is too much a product of inner resources and that pays too little attention to external necessities. Aiken needed to come to a more balanced view of the two extremes before he was to write his best poetry. He was at first in the position of the young hero of the short story, "Strange Moonlight" (in *Bring! Bring!,* 1925), who needed to come a long way before he knew what death really meant—that is, before he could isolate the word from its romantic associations and identify it with the facts of loss and absence and void.

It was a matter of coming to terms with these facts—and to the frequent abruptness and violence of their occasions—before the language would stop being merely brilliant, *un embarras de richesse.* But the basic qualities of mind were nevertheless there from the beginning: the sense of taste and limit (in the work of others as well as in his); the forceful belief in what he once inadequately described as a "subconscious treasure," that is, the emotive and conative resources of the poet; and the conviction that the basic modern "religion" is involved in the enhancement, the refinement, and the use of the human consciousness.

He has always enthusiastically endorsed "virtuosity," as his judgment of Delmore Schwartz and Dylan Thomas testifies (*Atlantic Monthly,* August, 1940; ABC, 93-103). He wishes to see "the poet once more standing, as he did in the Elizabethan age, naturally and vigorously at the center of the world" (ABC, 103). But this hope also means that the poet's stance is responsibly free of either self-indulgence or a too simple or too easy social commitment. It puts him in the responsible position of arbiter and shaping spirit, and it immensely raises his value.

Perhaps the best statement of Aiken's insight into the creative process comes not in a critical essay but in his last novel, *Conversation* (1940). The hero, Timothy Kane, a painter, husband, and father, finds each of the three roles threatened by a stupid though bitter quarrel. Searching for a rationalization of both art and love, he reflects that they emerge from the same source and the same desire: to bring matter formally to life. Where did a picture come from, he asks himself:

From a dream perhaps: from the bloodstream perhaps: from memory perhaps. . . . A nucleus smaller and brighter than a tear; and how astonishingly more fecund and powerful—the infinitesimal droplet of wild rain, wild water, growing, whirling, expanding, until it should become an all-containing sphere of creative and whirling light, a microcosm of living shape. . . .[16]

These reflections emphasize the drive toward consciousness that is stressed in Aiken's criticism. The urge to definition, to design, which is a fundamental fact of the artist's emotional life, is a form of the imagination pushing out toward the world of matter, creatively reshaping it, remaking it. ". . . And one's love too, was that not there also? *Must* it not be there? As of the first leaf that one ever loved, the first sunbeam one ever saw on a wall, or on the coarse bark of a tree, the first rain that one ever walked out into alone . . ." (*Conversation*, 161).

Both art and humanity are "at one and the same time, of love and terror" (161). The love and the terror exist in conflict, in tension, in balance, throughout his work. They are maneuvered into a brilliant variety of aesthetic forms and balances: in fantasy, in comical or pathetic human exchanges, in elaborate "musical schemata, or in "preludes to definition."

CHAPTER 2

The Fictional Ego

I

IN HIS TRIBUTE to Conrad Aiken in the special issue of *Wake*, Malcolm Lowry vigorously objected to *Time's* pronouncement that "it is for his short stories that Aiken is most likely to be remembered."

> That is, that while there's no reason why half a dozen of his short stories shouldn't survive, as among the best of their kind, it is extremely unlikely that a miscarriage of justice in the realm of enlightened criticism . . . should go for so long unredeemed into posterity as to result in the stories being remembered by future generations, while the magnificent body of poems was forgotten. . . .[1]

The fact is that Aiken did produce a considerable number of short stories to which he added five novels. Whether or not he will be "remembered" for these or for his poems, they are remarkably "of a piece," complementary to one another, and they come out of the same sources and beginnings. The differences of genre are of course noticeable, but the voice of the fiction is the voice of the poems. There is a "fictional ego" who undergoes as many variations as the ego informing the poems.

Through ten years of his career, Aiken alternated volumes of short stories with novels: 1925, *Bring! Bring! and Other Stories;* 1927, *Blue Voyage;* 1928, *Costumes by Eros;* 1933, *Great Circle;* 1934, *Among the Lost People;* and 1935, *King Coffin.* For the rest of the 1930's, he published two more novels (*A Heart for the Gods of Mexico*, 1939; *Conversation*, 1940); and in 1950 he published the majority of his short stories in a one-volume edition.[2]

scendentalism is his view of it as supraphenomenal:
mode of apprehension that transcended one's sensor
edge of the phenomenal world and all the experienc
senses. . . . It is interesting to notice, in this connecti
very flimsy and impractical, how absurdly and charming
cent, were such ideas of social awareness as this group
tained . . ." (ABC, 88-89).

But Aiken reserves his final judgment of the New E
mind for his remarks about Melville and Emily Dick
Moby Dick is "the final and perfect finial to the Puritan
perate three-century-long struggle with the problem of
There follows an analysis of the white whale symbol that p
from D. H. Lawrence's earlier study but is much more suc
and cogent. The ambivalence of "delight and terror," the d
lenge to moral awareness, the awful temptation (growing f
the Puritan moral concentration) for man to assert himself
above God: these are all here explosively presented and id
tified. *Moby Dick* marks the end of the special kinds of int
spection initiated by Puritan religious habits. In the poetry
Emily Dickinson the rhetoric of the New England manner
so individually self-contained as to bring it to a polite and discreet conclusion.

The intelligence of this survey reveals more than is at first
apparent. Aiken's view—a not unacceptable one—involves three
judgments: that the *personal* concentration upon man's specific
relationship to God became a celebration of self-prestige, and
transcendentalism made of it a way of denying tragedy; that
this denial eventually led to a crashing *dénouement*, in the conquest of Ahab by the White Whale; and finally, that the entire
question of a personal involvement in evil was set aside by late
nineteenth-century naturalism. The brilliance of Miss Dickinson's
ironies concerning the Puritan soul and God is a marginal and
concluding commentary.

These views of New England are relevant to any study of
Conrad Aiken's fiction. Their relevance is seldom bluntly evident, but it is true that the fiction presents several figures and
situations whose outlines are better seen in terms of the back-
ground I have sketched in above. There is the problem of discovery: the discovery of major facts (of death, ugliness, evil)
and of the disappearance of all easy evasions. Correspondingly,

Aiken represents the figure of the lonely child or old man (the "lost people" of his third volume) comprehending infinity within the limits of his own emotional economies.

There is also Aiken's own special version of the battle of the sexes: the almost infinite number of personal situations which help to define it almost always lead us to the edge of the eleven-year-old's discovery in Savannah. These stories have complementary themes: the corruptibility of the flesh, the temptations of the flesh, the haunting presence of ominous "sinfulness." Most directly related to Aiken's summary of the New England tradition are his sketches of the proud, lonely men (or, for that matter, the timid, lonely man), whose gaucheries feebly echo the major sounds of the New England past. These stories are among Aiken's least successful; the rationale tends to get in the way of the promise of three-dimensional writing.

The basic requirement of the Aiken story is the fact of human relationship. His fictional world is inhabited by persons at its center (not necessarily happily so) engaged in tense struggles for "understanding"; by persons moving from the edge to the center, in a voyage of emotional discovery; by persons far from the center, who have deliberately separated themselves from it, from a delusion of superiority; and by persons (usually the very young or the very old) who have left the center and are moving, alone and pitifully, toward "infinity." All of these figurations of the ego assume a basic aloneness—and of the kind suggested so often in Emily Dickinson's poems about God and "that gentleman guest," Death.

At his best, Aiken is a superb storyteller. He succeeds much more often in the short form than in the novel. His sharpness of observation and his insights into character momentarily "trapped" by his imagination seem more suitably adapted to the short story form. This is probably why the novels are often very good in certain passages but seldom so in "the long haul."

From the standpoint of the reader's watching the author compose (as distinguished from his remarking the finished composition), the story "Life Isn't a Short Story" serves as a remarkable laboratory.[7] As his story opens, the writer is discovered one morning in a cheap restaurant having his breakfast coffee and looking out at the passing scene. He has run out of ideas; despairs of ever writing another story; and stares idly at the street outside, with no confidence in it (for "life isn't a short story"). His interest is momentarily revived when he notices a middle-aged woman, "walking quickly, her umbrella pulled low over her head, so that the whiteness of her profile was sharp and immediate against the purple shadow." She is obviously purposeful and "real"; "she had come from somewhere and was going somewhere, and she was doing it with obvious concentration and energy" (*Short Stories*, 328).

Perhaps there is a story there? He had had an idea suggested to him some time before in the lobby of the "Orpheum Theatre," where he'd heard two very commonplace phrases: "as I live and breathe" and "in the flesh." Now he speculates upon their usefulness in a story; both obviously mean *alive:*

> . . . As I live and breathe—I am standing here living and breathing, you are standing there living and breathing, and it's a surprise and a delight to both of us. In the flesh, too—death hasn't yet stripped our bones, or the crematory tried out our fats. We haven't seen each other for a long while, we didn't know whether we were dead or not, but here we are.

In the very commonplaceness of the remarks lies their usefulness; they are universal testimonies of "aliveness," of the surprise and gratitude expressed through centuries of meetings that death had not yet caught up with us: "aeons of weather and aeons of handshake lay upon them; one witnessed, in the mere hearing of them, innumerable surprised greetings, innumerable mutual congratulations on the mere fact of being still alive" (*Short Stories*, 329-30).

But about "the blonde lady in Fitchburg," who was to be in his story? She wouldn't appreciate the echoing of these phrases, would in fact consider them vulgar. The middle-aged woman who had hurried through his field of vision set his mind working once again on his heroine. The details would be different, of course; the two women are not the same, but even so the "real" one had started a series of thoughts about the other. Gladys (a very suitable name) prides herself on her superiority to such vulgar commonplaces, and thus proves herself "the sort of hopelessly vulgar and commonplace person" who would manage her life in terms of stupid and small superiorities. Sidney, her husband, would exactly fit her idea of vulgarity. A person of little education and no "culture," he would, after the romance had worn off, irritate her again and again in "the deadly round of the merely quotidian" that followed (*Short Stories*, 330-31).

The writer's thoughts are interrupted by the facts of his own "merely quotidian" (a pair of "quickly sharp eyes" look momentarily at him through the window and then disappear); but he continues sketching the story in his mind. Gladys is, of course, a woman of "culture" and "learning"; she will read the *Christian Science Monitor* because "she liked to read about books and music and foreign affairs, and it frequently gave her ideas for little talks to the Women's Club." She would pose as a woman "tragically disillusioned" in love who had found "that love was dust and ashes and that men were—well, creatures of a lower order" (*Short Stories*, 333-34).

As the writer develops his heroine, he notes that it has begun to rain harder outside, that "people had begun to run, to scurry, in one's and two's and three's, exactly like one of those movies of the Russian Revolution, when invisible machine guns were turned on the crowds" (*Short Stories*, 336). A remarkable grace-note, this, for it provides a wry yet intense reflection upon the story taking shape in his mind. It is as though the story were taking place in two quite different kinds of tone: the stupid frivolities of Gladys; the penetrating insights into real terror and pity intruding upon the story itself—in fact, *making* it a story of some significance. The genius of Aiken's handling of both scenes is noted in the ways in which they move into and out of each other. Over all of it is the presiding sentiment expressed in the petty phrases "as I live and breathe" and "in the flesh." The presence of the thought of death, of death's imminence, pushed aside like the fact of God's scrutiny over man, returns in these "vulgar commonplaces."

The fictional world of Gladys and Sidney depends upon them. Her "refinement" is again and again to be offended by his recourse to "empty" banalities—until he will finally agree to give her a divorce, leaving her free of them. There will, of course, be an attempt at reconciliation, but it will collapse and fail when he says, "Well, as I live and breathe, if it isn't Gladys!" (*Short Stories*, 338).

In the end, the two scenes merge, or the imagined one fades into the real, as the writer sits staring out at a horse standing patiently in the hard rain (living and breathing) and waiting for the towel-supply man to order him on. "A long day was still ahead of him, a day of crowded and noisy streets, streets full of surprises and terrors and rain, muddy uneven cobbles and greasy smooth asphalt" (*Short Stories*, 339). This is a masterful story: at one and the same time, it is a story, the story of a story, and a series of scenic commentaries upon its meaning—each indispensable to the others; and the whole gives depth and vision, and a sense of gaiety.[8]

II

To take the kinds of human relationship I have mentioned above, but in a rather different order from that given there, I should like first to discuss the story of self-discovery, the child moving toward adulthood. The central experience of discovery is violence of some kind, a form of memory of the Savannah experience, though not a simple duplication of it. In the novels, Aiken's heroes are liable to "talk their way through" to discovery —as in Andy Cather's case of *Great Circle*, which will be discussed later. The stories of childhood are a different thing altogether. There is a sense of profound mystery involved, and the hero prefers to move quietly toward its dissolution.

"Strange Moonlight" is an example. The young hero moves in an atmosphere vague, dark, and mysterious toward the answer to a simple question: what is death? At first he thinks of it only as "absence"; someone who was there once is now no longer there. He is obviously a precocious youth, much involved in inner fantasies. His child's mind is at first reassured by presences; then it is upset by an absence. Little Caroline Lee has died. How could anyone he had actually known *die?* "Mystery was once more about him, the same mystery that had shone in the vision of the infernal city. . . ."[9]

The way to discovery is through his parents, whose characterization is much indebted to Aiken's own parents. There is the scene (repeated almost exactly in the autobiographical *Ushant*) of the parents' odd mixture of quarreling and loving at the same time. After observing this situation, he has an imaginary conversation with Caroline Lee, about dying:

". . . it's really quite easy—you just hold your breath and shut
your eyes."
"Oh!"
"And when you're lying there, after you've died, you're really
just pretending. You keep very still, and you have your eyes
almost shut, but really you know everything! You watch the
people and listen to them" (*Bring! Bring!*, 47).

This exchange is obviously indebted to the hero's reading of
Poe's stories; for the idea of retaining consciousness after death,
and of being somehow superior to the living, is a Poe grotesque.
    Subsequently, the family go on a beach picnic, and the children
"bury" their father; only his head is left out of the sand. Wasn't
this, after all, like Caroline Lee's description of being dead?
His father was there, alive in his grave, "and talking, and able to
get up whenever he liked" (53). But the boy has yet to come
out of the "strange moonlight" of his dreams and recognize death
for what it is. The discovery occurs on the return home.

> The long street, in the moonlight, was like a deep river, at the
> bottom of which they walked, making scattered, thin sounds on
> the stones. . . . He stared up at this while his father fitted the
> key into the lock, feeling the ghostly vine grow strangely over
> his face and hands. Was it in this, at last, that he would find the
> explanation of all that bewildered him? Caroline, no doubt,
> would understand it; she was a sort of moonlight herself . . .
> (*Bring! Bring!*, 55).

It is through the moonlight, with its silences and softnesses,
that he finally comes to realize that Caroline is dead, and what
death is, after all. It is a sense of emptiness, of being deprived
of all animation, sounds, even solid vision of objects. This is the
vision of a child who must translate from the imaginary to the
real, even though both have aspects that are strangely alike.
    Conrad Aiken's analysis of the child's sense of separation
from his surroundings and of his curious dependence upon and
yet isolation from the adult world is here very competently presented. There is a sense of premonition. The conception of death
is as much associated with his father (who is "buried" in the
sand and remains superior to the event) as it is with his companion, who has actually died. Like the old man who is on the
way to death (Mr. Arcularis, Mr. Smith of *Blue Voyage*, etc.),

the child suffers a sense of deprivation that comes from a failure of experience. But the most famous of Aiken's child sensibilities is the hero of "Silent Snow, Secret Snow."[10]

This story begins, as does "Strange Moonlight," with a mystery partly invented, at least willfully encouraged and prolonged. The great difference is that in "Silent Snow, Secret Snow" it is never allowed to "break" against the facts. "It was as if, in some delightful way, his secret gave him a fortress, a wall behind which he could retreat into heavenly seclusions" (*Lost People*, 128). In school, while Miss Buell tells him and his fellow students about the tropics, he remains within the cold securities of the Arctic and Antarctic. Night after night the vision of the secret snow increases; he wills that it shut off all human sounds, and he measures each morning how remote it makes the sound of the postman's steps, ". . . as if removed by one degree from actuality—as if everything had been insulated by snow" (*Lost People*, 132). It pleased him that there should be no actual snowfall, that the snow should remain secret—his own willed conceit hiding the ugly world.

Inevitably the separation brings him into a clash with his parents. How keep a balance between the two worlds? It was becoming increasingly difficult to make the leap from one into the other; it was easier and more tempting to remain in the world of his own imagining. "At whatever pain to others, nevertheless, one must persevere in severance, since the incommunicability of the experience demanded it . . ." (*Lost People*, 142).

Finally the "severance" is complete. He breaks angrily from his parents and the doctor, who are trying to intrude into his mystery; and, as he re-enters his room, "a cold low humming shook the windows." The snow enters his room; it is suddenly, terribly disturbed by a "gash of horrible light," his mother's opening the door, which forces it to draw back, hissing. Turning to his mother, he shouts to her to go away—he hates her. And, with that, the matter is settled.

> . . . everything was solved, everything became all right: the seamless hiss advanced once more, the long white wavering lines rose and fell like enormous whispering sea-waves, the whisper becoming louder, the laughter more numerous.
>
> . . . .
>
> —the whole world was a vast moving screen of snow—but even

now it said peace, it said remoteness, it said sleep (*Lost People*, 157).

This story is the most sensational, as it is the most memorable, of those about Aiken's "lost people." The narrative consistently stays within the boy's mind, moving with it toward his destruction, never suggesting or stating reasons or trying to probe "psychologically" into the boy's injured spirit. It is a psychic scene of remarkable purity; the adult world stays always dimly at the fringe of the boy's awareness and of his sense of his relationship. What has caused the aberration is never revealed, but his desire to withdraw from human communication is faithfully followed to its ultimate, total rejection of the family and submission to the vision.

The snow is death, or the means to death, a confrontation of infinity or of natural immensities. The special quality of Aiken's personal tragedies is that they involve, or state, or suggest such confrontations. *Among the Lost People* has a number of such portraits. Its "editorial" piece is the sketch "Gehenna,"[11] which defines the tortures of isolation developed elsewhere. However varied the sketches are, there is a core of frightened loneliness or madness in each of them. The spirit of Edgar Allan Poe hovers over some of them (and, occasionally, the style as well). For the most part, however, the stories are psychologically self-sufficient. The strangely mad, religious hero of "Bow Down, Isaac!" is clearly motivated by an obsessive attention to the word of the Lord, and he is punished in the end in a way consistent to his reading of that word.

Not all of the stories are successful. Occasionally, as in "No, No, Go Not to Lethe" (one of those Aiken had the wisdom not to include in the 1950 *Short Stories*), he is so anxiously after "his point" that the demonstration of it is without life or skill.

One of the volume's marked successes is "Mr. Arcularis."[12] It has actually assumed three versions: the short story, as it appears in this collection; the play *Fear No More*, as it was performed in England (adapted and directed by Diana Hamilton); and the published play,[13] in which Aiken restored some of the ideas that had been rejected for the public performance.

In his introduction to the published play, Aiken explains the development of the "Arcularis" idea. He had met a Mr. Arcularis, an "odd, pale, shabby little man, who by chance sat opposite me, years ago, at the dinner-table—Third Class—of an Atlantic liner. . . . almost from the outset I thought of him as somehow having the air of a somnambulist, a sleepwalker . . ." (*Mr. Arcularis*, v). The actual Arcularis was easily enough translated into the fictional one, who first appeared in T. S. Eliot's *Criterion* magazine.

Then an Englishwoman, who had once been married to Sutton Vane, author of the play *Outward Bound*, a successful adaptation of a similar idea, proposed to adapt "Mr. Arcularis" to the stage. She and her assistants had some odd ideas about the means necessary to a successful conversion; they needed, as they said, to "thicken the plot" and did so by providing poor Arcularis with a nagging, shrewish wife, who was to haunt him from and to the grave: ". . . this sinister and wholly implausible person, like something out of Dracula, was supposed to have mesmeric powers over her husband, powers which she exercised only for evil" (vii-viii). Aiken countered by giving him instead a mother who directed his actions from the grave. And it was this final version, *sans* wife and with "the faithless and beautiful mother," that found its way into print and into a trial-run performance at the "Arena Stage," Washington, D. C. (1951).

This history of the several mutations of Arcularis has its own virtues. In the story, he is a lonely old man, about to die, with no personal associations aside from those attending his last hospital rites. He is entirely "on his own," and his motivations are like those of many of Aiken's other *personae*, the melancholy though courageous ones of facing the blank immensities without aid or prop or guide. The addition of a shrew to the plans for a public performance is understandable enough, though at what cost to Aiken's original conception of Mr. Arcularis we may only speculate.

What is most interesting of all, however, is that in redoing the play to his own taste Aiken should not have eliminated the "thickening" but only changed the character of it and added to it an idea from the novel *Great Circle*. It is an example in literature of the "great circle" move from art to experience and back to art; only in this case, instead of a move from Boston to Savannah to "infinity," it is a (disguised) curve from Boston to the Atlantic to Kentucky to death.

Aiken is preoccupied with the problems of "coming to terms" with destiny. In the short story, Mr. Arcularis has only to come to terms with death and the move into annihilating immensities of space; but in the play, he must accept the "terror" of some violent event in his childhood before he can accept the accompanying horror of his own death. It is a strange inversion of psychotherapy; a deathbed reconciliation with a dead mother obstructs the way to his facing the impersonal, blank reaches of the descent to death.

The simplicity of the original story has its own charms. Mr. Arcularis, apparently just recovered from a serious operation, is ordered by his doctor to go on a sea voyage; the secret of his real voyage (he is all the while on the operating table, and the sea voyage is actually a voyage into death) is not divulged until the very end, though in both versions of the play it is rather crudely and bluntly forced immediately upon the attention of the audience.

Weak to the point of giddiness, Arcularis "found himself smiling foolishly at everything" (*Lost People*, 15); the humming and throbbing of the ship's engines seemed to match the rhythm of his pain. The rhythms are to be duplicated in the effects of his dreams on successive nights (obviously intended to match the movements toward and away from consciousness in the actual experience of the operating theatre). Each time in his dream he was to move far out into cosmic spaces: "He tinkled and spangled in the void, hallowed to the waste echoes, rounded the buoy on the verge of the unknown, and tacked glitteringly homeward. . ." (*Lost People*, 30).

Each time, when he returns, he is left terrified and alone; but the ship's doctor reassures him, and the person who "happens to be along" says that these things always come from a sense of guilt: "You feel guilty about something. I won't be so rude as to inquire what it is. But if you could rid yourself of the sense of guilt—" (*Lost People*, 33). The guilt is not specified, and is not intended to be; it is much more accurately in line with Aiken's having transformed his own "sense of guilt" or sense of terror into the cosmic naturalism of his poetic search for definition. It is perhaps too much to expect that Mr. Arcularis will have the courage of Aiken's poetry; but in the original story, he is a symbol of pure loneliness, separated from other persons

except in the most casual associations and dependent upon no one but himself for help in facing the voids that death is opening to him.

As he dreams, he also sleepwalks—or crawls on his hands and knees, moving toward the coffin he knows is in the hold (one of the stewards had told him there "was a corpse aboard"). In his final "voyage," he achieves a phenomenal, supernatural speed: "In no time at all he was beyond the moon, shot past the North Star as if it were standing still (which perhaps it was?), swooped in a long, bright curve round the Pleiades, shouted his frosty greetings to Betelgeuse, and was off to the little blue star which pointed the way to the Unknown . . ." (*Lost People*, 42). This time he does not return: "The surgeon's last effort to save Mr. Arcularis's life had failed" (43). The voyage has finally extended into infinity itself, into death; he is at last, and terribly, alone.

In its original form this fantasy has a certain distinction that gives it an "isolated glory" in Aiken's fictional work. In almost every other case, he is arranging motivations; "Silent Snow, Secret Snow" is an exception, but here we may "reconstruct" a motive by staying patiently within the boy's mind. Mr. Arcularis, however, is a poetic, secular "everyman" on the voyage to nullity. Were it not for a pervasive sentiment (the nurses, companions, doctors show "sympathy" and are distressed in conventional ways), "Mr. Arcularis" might be called an American version of the Beckett hero.

In the play, however, the story is too much dominated by the atmospheres of the hospital and the nursery. The voyage to cosmic nothingness is superintended too anxiously and persistently. The play opens as it closes, with Arcularis supine on an operating table, a "frame" of infinity, I suppose, but a much too obvious one. In Act II, Scene 3, his mother and Uncle David call out to him from the "Great Circle" beyond home, and he is obliged to confess his fears of past experiences (*Mr. Arcularis*, 63-64). These are almost identical to those to which Andrew Cather returns in the novel *Great Circle* (1933), but they are there skillfully treated and "right." The rest of the play is an "explanation" of his mother and his Uncle David which prepares Arcularis for his own death through condemning theirs. The confession out of the past and Arcularis's death combine at

the last, crucial moment, and he goes to his own death purged
of the terror that had pursued him in life.

III

The figure of Andy Cather (*Great Circle*) somehow mediates
between the heroes of "Silent Snow, Secret Snow" and "Mr. Arcularis." Like them, he is a displaced soul, but unlike either (if we
forget the dramatized version of Arcularis) he comes to us fully
equipped with reasons, causes, and therapeutic suggestions. We
discover him at the novel's beginning on the train from New
York, hurrying back to Boston and Cambridge because he has
been "tipped off" in the matter of his wife's adultery.

Not only his train but he himself is racing; the pace of the
opening chapter suggests an acceleration of feeling to the verge
of hysteria: "You are deliberately seeking a catastrophe—you
are yourself in the act of creating a disaster. . . ."[14] In the taxi
on the way to Cambridge, Cather's progress is momentarily
halted by police investigation of a suicide in the Charles River.
"In the taxi again, he lit a cigarette, and noticed that his hands
were trembling. Good God, was this a symbol, a kind of warn-
ing? Cling to life, you poor bastard . . ." (*Great Circle*, 37-38).

The pace of his voyage to discovery is furious; it is actually,
at this point, a voyage to the first phase of self-recognition. It
swirls and spirals up and dips down, and it is accompanied
by a torrent of disjointed and irrational phrases which flood
his brain. Characteristic are the obscenities he heaps upon his
view and memory of sex: "Sex! Good jumping Jesus, to think of
the nuisance, and nothing but nuisance, that sex had been. And
after all this time, after a hundred years, at half-past nine, or
half-past God, this final climax. This banal climax" (*Great
Circle*, 45).

But it is not to be a climax, only an awkward and terrible
beginning of the act of self-discovery. There are to be many
other "banal climaxes" and headaches, and hangovers, and loud
selfish quarrels and pitiful self-defenses. Out of the fear of
making it "banal," Cather shouts at his wife:

> . . . You don't know what love is. You're a thirteen-year-old
> romantic, a bleached little Cantabrigian Madame Bovary. I want
> love, she cries, and pulls on a pair of tarpaulin knickers.

—Shut up! She turned suddenly and glared at him, her mouth dreadfully relaxed, the tears starting quickly from her eyes. He was looking at her quite coldly, with the familiar hatred, the familiar deep ferocity and need to injure . . . (*Great Circle*, 69).

Andy Cather, moved to his Club, very drunk, struggling between nausea and unconsciousness, sinks all the way into a dream which carries him back to his childhood. It is the childhood of Mr. Arcularis in the version of the published play: there are mother and Uncle David and the yacht; and there is the storm in which they are drowned, left there for him to discover dead. It is the lurid combination of the two uglinesses, of adultery and death, that has haunted him all these years and made a shambles of his own marriage.

Part II of *Great Circle* is beautifully handled. As it begins, we see the consciousness of Andy Cather being sucked down into the memory of his youth: "—particularly the smell of the pinewood walls, soaked in sea-fog, but pine-smelling also in the strong sea sunlight, smooth to the touch, golden-eyed with knotholes, and the wind singing through the rusty wire screens, fine-meshed and dusty, or clogged brightly with drops of dew, or drops of rain, or drops of fog . . ." (*Great Circle*, 86). It is here, in the summer, on the coast, that the tragedy develops: his father estranged, living apart; his Uncle David "acting funny" and being very sporty with his mother; he himself forced to pretend he knows nothing about it, but actually painfully trying to puzzle his way through it; the sense of desperate loss, or the imminence of loss; and the great mystery of the family's suddenly being awkwardly pulled apart. Andy is "back there," having come the great circle through his dream, revisiting and reliving the puzzling and tragic experience.

. . . Pretending we didn't know anything. Pretending, pretending, pretending. I was sick of pretending. First from Father, and then from Mother, and then from Susan. What was the use. My sneakers were wet with walking through the wet grass, they began to bubble, I felt the cold bubbles under the naked soles of my feet and swished them though the thick weeds and grass beside the path to fill them and refill them with cold water . . . (*Great Circle*, 146).

When the tragedy does occur, Cather is the one to find the bodies. They are undignified in their deaths, and they are horribly together—as they shouldn't have been, even when they were alive. "I wished they hadn't put Mother and Uncle David in the same room. And would Father come down to Duxbury now—" (181). But Andy Cather must come back, to his own adulthood, to the terrible mess and mystery of it, having scarcely solved the mystery left over from childhood.

In Chapter III, we find him in the apartment of a psychoanalyst friend. Here the struggle to understand reaches its crucial stage. He fights the dream, the necessities of the present, the jargon of psychoanalysis, his own sense of guilt, above all the pain of his double hurt. "An unreasoning terror, a terror that had no particular shape . . ." (197). He is always dreaming of the sea, trying to become a child again. The closer he comes to that admission, the nearer he is to confessing the basic source of his trouble. But the journey is not easy or simple; he resents his friend's easy manipulations of his problem into technical language and definition.

Gradually, slowly, the secret is revealed. He is disgusted by the "filthy intimacy" of marriages, this matter of knowing the body too well (239). This disgust is of course closely, intimately associated with the shock of childhood, the adulterous mother destroying the family through her self-indulgence. Love, he says, is "nothing on earth but a domestication of death. Our little domestic death . . ." (260). Then, his friend gone, Cather sinks into a sodden sleep, now into a dream not just of memory but of the full, intimate realization of the terror.

The dream will purge him of the terror: ". . . *this strange house where Bertha lives and all our children and all our relatives . . .*" (286). All personal relationships are now confused. It is the deepest descent Andy is ever to make: everything is grotesque, distorted; the "face like jelly," a man's head, "*and this face is watching them dry watching them die . . . watching the tide go out and see the agony on that face the lips contorted in hatred and scorn . . .*" (290). It is the dead face of his Uncle David, the face of his father, but most of all his own face as he watches the dead bodies and as he watches the faces of his wife and friends move and "die" away from him.

When he awakens, when he comes "upward from the dark world through the wild sheets of light" (298), he is on the way to being "cured." "You in the flesh again, redivivus . . ."

(303). There are a few hard tasks ahead, but he feels an immense relief. He must now go back to Duxbury, alone, to see if he can actually face it and accept it; but the assumption is that he will and that, the journey made, he will return to his adult life an adult man.

It is difficult to convey the intricacy of *Great Circle*. Looking back upon it, we find scarcely a wasted thought or image or sentence. It is so successfully linked to the human situation that passages that may appear at first to be exercises in "virtuosity" end by being superbly relevant. Perhaps it is too much to expect that this "case" of Andrew Cather will prove to be a great novel; but it is a much underrated work. Seen in the perspective of Aiken's other work, and after a fresh reading of it, what appear at first impression to be "frantic images" are acceptable as one of the most precise descriptions of the imagery of fright and terror.

The pace, frantic at the beginning, terrifyingly slow at its first crisis, eases into that of a young boy's walk along the sand of a beach to his father, or from his father to the awful scene of the storm and his mother's corpse. Then it picks up once more: Andy quickly, evasively sliding away from his friend's advices, shouting and screaming out of his compounded injury. Finally, the novel plunges into the abysses of his unconscious, where all of the details of the two scenes are chaotically mixed, until he rises from them, as from the dead.

Great Circle belongs to the cycle of fictions associated with the "lost people." It was published within a year of the collection called *Among the Lost People;* and it also belongs (if we look at Aiken's other major genre of work) to the period of the Preludes, the poems in which he is seeking over and over again for the precise words to define his relationship to chaos and death: as observer, participator, victim, transcendent artist.

The soul of Andy Cather is "saved," and for that fact I suppose we may feel grateful. But it is not salvation but self-knowledge that is important here. Except for "Silent Snow, Secret Snow," Aiken's best works have a "recognition" scene—a scene in which, whether specifically or not, his protagonist sees into an abyss and identifies himself in relation to it. The moment may be at the edge of death, as it is in the story "Mr. Arcularis." Or it may come in one of the great circular sweeps through memory and the past that are characteristic of Cather's voyage toward discovery. This action, this type of movement, is similar to the dialectic of Aiken's best poems, many of which he was writing at the time of *Great Circle*.

IV

In a group of lesser (some of them quite inferior) stories, Conrad Aiken explores the superficies of death and evil—somewhat in the manner of the lavish melancholy of the poetry of *Charnel Rose* (1918). Here death is dust in a bowl of roses, or the rose itself withering before the eyes; evil is a mask to conceal the good. There is much melodramatic villainy. Aiken seems often to be working from contrivance; there is little elaboration, and the characters take on their roles before they have themselves been convincingly developed. There is more than a slight suggestion of Poe, as there is in the early poetry: effects are elaborated beyond usefulness or used without an attempt to define.

The preoccupation with death is not in itself illegitimate. We have already seen that it can be the basis of skillful and effective work. If the seriousness of the condition is clearly associated with a well-defined human economy, the results are often remarkably successful. There is a slight though momentarily interesting situation in "The Last Visit,"[15] an affecting story of the heroine's trip to see her grandmother for the last time. The old woman lies in a room of a private rest home, which is grotesquely and pitifully decorated with cheap religious prints on the walls and cheap rugs on the floor: "Above the mantel, Christ was leaning down, much haloed, into the valley of the shadow of death, reaching an incredibly long arm to rescue a lost lamb: over the dark valley hung a dove with bright wings. A pot of ferns stood on a small high bamboo table near the piano: the piano was a florid affair of pale oak . . ." (*Bring! Bring!*, 176). The grandmother, herself so far gone on the journey to death, is desperately irritated that she hasn't yet achieved it: "'I can't die! I can't die! . . . I want to die and I can't!'" She cried almost soundlessly, the tears running down the wrinkles of her cheeks . . ." (183).

It is precisely this close identity of scene with person that makes the story effective. But there are times when Aiken takes his eyes off the scene, tries to "prove something" about which he has not made up his mind or fixed in the angle of his vision. The results are uniformly mediocre. This is the case with "By My Troth, Nerissa!"[16] in which the hero, haunted by thoughts of worms and corruption, writes a letter to his sweetheart: ". . . Why is it that you are made of flesh—Why, indeed, if God, as it is reported, created you in His image, did He not dispense for once with the common straw and clay and dip His hands into the clear brightness of the ether? . . ." (*Bring! Bring!*, 95-96).

This obsession with death involves a direct opposition of it to beauty; the hero wishes to hide from temporality in some kind of eternity, but he cannot rid himself of the image of the corpse that replaces the beauty that is now. When he meets Sara, he breaks out in a fury over her sweet reasonableness.

> "Don't be so damned reasonable! Only death is reasonable."
> He saw Sara looking at him with fright, as if she saw something horrible in his face. What did she see? A sharp green-lit vision of him hanging from a gas fixture? . . . A torrent of grief seemed to be released within him, he felt a quickening sensation in his tear-ducts; and, tightly clasping Sara's forearm with his hand, he started walking again (103).

The novel *A Heart for the Gods of Mexico*[17] is a very different conception; or, rather, it is several ideas brought together and displayed. Its major objective is to describe a death; but Aiken, choosing the setting deliberately, moves the invalid from Boston to D. H. Lawrence's and Hart Crane's Mexico so that she may die more spectacularly. It is almost as though he had contrived a plot in order to give himself and the reader a journey across middle and western America. Whatever the motive, the novel has many passages of mystery—even of terror—that are closely associated with the reality of a quickly changing scene.

Noni, a beautiful and wonderfully kind woman, wishes to remarry before her heart ailment conquers her; but she needs a quick Mexican divorce to win the race with death. Inadequately financed, the journey of the three (Noni; Blomberg, a friend; and Gil, the fiancé) has to be managed in coach trains, with great difficulties and mysterious early morning schedule changes. The novel is memorable for the geography it reveals along the way, on that "centripetal and tumultuous descent into the Inferno. . . . All day, all night, the landscape whirling and unfolding and again folding, rising and falling, swooping and melting, opening and shutting . . ." (*Heart*, 47, 51). The train moves through Hart Crane's midland (of "The River")[18] with a sense of unlimited space transmuted into "Time with a hundred hands, time with a thousand mouths!" (71). The Mississippi River is "A whole continent pouring itself out lavishly to the sea, in superb everlasting waste . . ." (91).

The party moves into Mexico, and the sense of the grotesque increases, poor Noni's heart protesting and apparently about to give up the struggle. In the third-class car, "Derisive and demoniacal laughter, full of fierce and abandoned hatred, the pride of pridelessness, the arrogance of the self-condemned . . ." (110). Almost in the spirit of a Lawrencean heroine, Noni approaches the "altar" of the Mexican gods to offer her heart. The end comes soon after their arrival in Cuernavaca, a weird, tilting city high in the mountains, where the hot sun alternates with torrential rains. Blomberg, watching this beloved woman dying, is outraged by the senselessness not only of the journey but generally of the universe itself.

> [Noni's death] was a votive offering: there could be no doubt about that: it was, as he remembered now, a throwing of flowers into the sea: and that a life should have been so beautiful, and so devoted to good and beautiful things, in the face of the uncompromising principles of impermanence and violence, came to him as a fierce renewal of his faith in the essential magnificence of man's everlasting defeat . . . (*Heart*, 151).

Blomberg is the "almost pure" Aiken hero. Gentle, persuasive, cultivated, sensitive, he goes on a journey; while it is a land journey this time, it is also a "great circle," a curve of motion toward an ineluctably tragic end. Here the hero superintends, or chaperones perhaps, the voyage to death in a setting "as meaningless as a tomb" (155). There is nothing of Lawrence's furious denial of the "mental civilization" here, nor of his celebration of dark gods. Conrad Aiken does not go in for such emotional overtones to pagan ceremonies. His hero and heroine move through the darkness and the terror and wonder of a continent inevitably; and when the end comes (so, so far from the Boston Common), the survivor reaffirms a bewildering faith in man's "essential magnificence."

A Heart for the Gods of Mexico is something less than a complete realization of what Aiken wants to give. It is much taken over by the emotional dynamics of its geographical scene. Nevertheless, there are many signs of an aborted promise. The book might have been truly remarkable if the reader did not consume so much time reading between the lines of a travel folder. The hero and heroine are too much occupied looking at scenes to be centrally involved in them. But they have a genuineness that almost comes through in spite of their limited opportunity. Eventually, they are both swamped by their own, and Aiken's, rhetoric.

They are persons on the edge of annihilation, not very much unlike E. A. Robinson's "Man Against the Sky" (though Aiken condemned that poem as too abstractly remote from human particulars); and they select their poses and gestures for the unreasonable ceremony of their disintegration. The villain of Aiken's fictional world is far less convincing. Briefly defined, he is the withdrawn, arrogant, self-centered, and often stupidly naïve person who makes an "experiment" of both living and dying. There is sometimes a mixture of Poe and of Dostoevsky in his makeup: Poe, in the sense of his curious fascination for the rank odors of evil; Dostoevsky, in the arrogant assumption of himself as of a higher moral order.

"The Letter" is an unfortunate case in point.[19] "I am a heartless creature, and I know it," he begins (*Bring! Bring!*, 186). While he avoids intimacies, he has "a private and all-devouring *curiosity* as to the lives, the intimate secret feelings, of others . . ." (189). A *voyeur* of human emotions, he delights in observing ("scientifically," of course) the agonies of others. At one time he pilfers a letter from someone who claims he will die of tuberculosis within two years. "Could there be a more exquisite case of what I mentioned as that instinct for exhibitionism, tremulously erotic, which underlies every friendship?" (20). To fulfill his expectations, he goes to the man's address, fully anticipating the sight of a man at death's edge. To his horror, the man in his suburban garden looks disgustingly healthy and is apparently looking forward to many more years.

Occasionally, Aiken tries to provide his version of the Gogol,

Dostoevsky's bureaucratic little man who is withdrawn not because of arrogance but timidity. Such a person is the narrator of "The Escape from Fatuity."[20] A bachelor, he is anxious to gain esteem and good will, but is too *shy;* as for women, he adores them, "but they terrify me" (*Bring! Bring!,* 122). He imagines himself having exotic adventures, but finds that he is only excusing himself for his fatuity, and he drowns his self-loathing in whiskey. This negligible character is the extreme example of the defeating introspection the Aiken hero often strives to conquer—perhaps most fully explored in the stream of consciousness of William Demarest of *Blue Voyage*. But Demarest is close to being a "whole" person, and these characters are only half-persons.

Aiken once divided the human personality in two; "Smith and Jones"[21] are his Jekyll and Hyde, the id and ego of this pitifully inadequate characterization. Smith, "vulgar," violent, obtrusive and boorish, embarrasses Jones repeatedly with his "persistent, unreflective low-grade sort of way" (*Bring! Bring!,* 116). The lovely and the obscene are hopelessly entangled; the rose is "charnel."

". . . I spoke, didn't I, of the beautiful obscene, and of the inextricable manner in which the two qualities are everywhere bound up together? The beautiful and the obscene. The desirable and the disgusting. I also compared this state of things with an organism in which a cancer was growing—which one tries to excise . . ." (116-17).

In the ensuing fracas, Jones kills the Smith in him, but of course in so doing makes him forever a part of himself: the criminal act is the Smith in him turning against itself. As he walks back to the city, he has a sense of always having been alone. "One would have said, at the moment, that he looked like a tramp" (119).

If I seem to have been overlong in describing Aiken's failures, it is only with the aim of setting the stage for a discussion of his major failure—in fiction, that is. All of the contrivances, half-starts, hollowness and thinness of characterization culminate in the novel *King Coffin*.[22] Its hero, Jasper Ammen, descends from Dostoevsky, Poe, and Nietzsche; and, in each case, he loses much from the inheritance. He will live beyond the ugly touch and sight of ordinary morals. He is a culmination, a "Zarathustrian," end-product of human evolution; his face is "the conscious end of the conscious world" (*Coffin*, 20); he takes a special pleasure in "hitting" and "hurting," a "special sharp delight in all duplicity" (26).

On the edge of Harvard Yard, Ammen plots the "perfect crime." The whole impetus for it must be *concentric*, "an affair of his own, a mere matter of revolving within or around himself . . ." (33). He is the Emersonian soul gone sour, an Ahab turned Raskolnikov, with the motive of neither for planning his acts.

He had at first joined a "leftist" group, a shabby affair; since he feels a Gulliver among Lilliputians (37), he resigns from them to withdraw into his "Nietzschean egoism" (49) to avoid the dangers of the commonplace. This strange pseudo-Nietzschean (who follows the popular misconception rather than the actual teachings of Nietzsche) abhors pity and humanity, and he proposes to himself to kill (at random, without personal motive) a representative nonentity.

Searching at length, he finally comes upon him in a subway car going to Boston. He is—marvel of marvels—not a Kosciusko nor a Blathington, but a simple *Jones*, an advertising man, middle-aged, with a very small business and apparently all of the middle-class virtues Ammen despises. Jones is the "one-who-wants-to-be-killed" (*Coffin*, 121), "the anonymous one, the abstract one, the mere Specimen Man . . ." (130). The perfect logic of his discovery requires an act of pure, unmotivated destruction, "the only natural purification" (195).

So much for his intent. Ammen is to discover unusual complications. Humanity intervenes. Jones is to be despised, of course; but isn't there a danger that he will also be pitied, even loved? Ammen reads his way into Jones's life and soul; the mistake is to assume that any human being can remain forever immune from contact with another. At the theatre one night, he sits near Jones and observes him: obviously a stupid man, who laughs at stale vaudeville jokes, and therefore bears "unconscious testimony to the perfection and necessity of the idea and the action" (*Coffin*, 249). He is the perfect—the almost "sacred"—scapegoat. But there is suddenly a message for Jones, and he leaves the theatre hastily. Could he have been tipped off by one of Ammen's enemies about his danger? No, hardly; he is on his way home where his wife is (prematurely) suffering birth pangs.

Jasper Ammen, who has let himself into the Jones basement, hears the screams of the ordeal above, notes the human disorder of the basement, hesitates and wonders. Could so stupid and simple a matter of human life thwart his superb plans? The child is stillborn, a fact that adds to the complication. Couldn't one say that nature has itself committed the crime? Isn't Jones now perfectly mocked for his human simplicities? The death of one who was not even born! Ammen now feels that the plan had gone sour, that it was no longer *"quite his own"* (*Coffin*, 301). When he telephones Jones to arrange a meeting, he finds Jones's voice hurried and preoccupied with his own sorrows; and this, too, is upsetting to Ammen (315).

Jasper hovers at the edge of the funeral in the "city of the dead"; the little parcel of not quite achieved humanity is buried before his eyes; and Ammen "felt that he had died" (336). So the novel ends. Though nothing is said, he has apparently given up his plan; in fact, he is emotionally distraught over having temporarily left the human race. He has apparently found something distinctive, something not quite anonymous, in Jones's plight; and, in finding it, he has discovered himself—as one of those souls who have scarcely the chance to say "I" before they die.

V

The collection of stories *Costumes By Eros*,[23] suitably introduced by a fragment of Othello's words to Desdemona (". . . and when I love thee not, / Chaos is come again"), testifies at some length and in some detail to Conrad Aiken's concern with the waywardness and eccentricity and indispensability of love. The stories here range widely, perhaps accounting for as many adventures and misadventures as any of their contemporaries. There are prostitutes and men on holiday, hopeful young girls, and disappointed young men. The sexual relationship is approached, denied, granted, enjoyed, lost; it is mysterious, becomes excitingly real, diminishes, and becomes tedious. The stories comprehend as wide a range of excellence as those in Aiken's other two volumes.

The most "depraved" of Aiken's heroines is, however, from another volume. She is Coralyn, "that gallantest of creatures," of "Thistledown."[24] A pretty girl, intelligent, ready and eager for love, she is first courted by the husband of the woman who has hired her as secretary. The man, who serves as a kind of aging Nick Carraway narrator throughout the story, at once notices her charm, but finds her also "very detached, very cynical, very passionate, but also very remote . . ." (*Lost People,* 256).

With a vivacious hardness and unpredictability, Coralyn rivals the best of Fitzgerald's heroines; as the anxious "older man" observes from a distance, "She thought men as a race were detestable, conceited, boring creatures, interesting only because they are so naively and disingenuously unscrupulous" (268). Her inevitable fate, to which she goes in a succession of leaps, happens in spite of the narrator's heroic efforts to "spare her." In the end, she has run the gamut of affairs, respecting no men and corrupting them all; and when the narrator sees her for the last time, "She looked appalling—quite literally appalling. Her face was a ghastly white, except for its deliberate scarlets; she was shabbily overdressed; and there was a new furtive something in her bearing . . ." (281-82).

The uncertain wavering between love and hatred, shyness and bravado, gallantry and gaucherie, which characterizes the love of man and woman, is analyzed in every detail in *Costumes By Eros.* "Field of Flowers,"[25] for example, has its hero in an affair with a married woman who has temporarily escaped her husband in Akron; the lover decides finally that she is not worth the trouble and expense of the affair, that she is shallow and insensitive. So the beautiful Hiroshige print he has exultingly found as a parting gift for her is in the end withheld; she is not worthy of that exquisite beauty.

More pitiful—though scarcely much more successfully portrayed—is the anguish of the exiled father of "I Love You Very Dearly,"[26] who has given up his family life to try again in Paris. He frankly confesses he has failed in his marriage; he is "a misfit, a second-rater" (*Eros,* 218). But he must advise his daughter on her marriage: "'. . . I want you to be happy; and all this nonsense, and this blather of confession of my own worthlessness, will be excused maybe if it helps you out'" (*Eros,* 224).

Much more in the mood of "lost people" is the figure of "A Man Alone at Lunch,"[27] who is pathetically counting his pennies, preparing for an operation, and fearing that he will lose his woman from inability to support her. His thought alternates between the desire to escape altogether (half-willing his death) and the hope that the operation will leave him sound and solvent and able to care for her. Another view of the sadness of love is to be found in one of Aiken's several descriptions of shipboard romances, "Farewell! Farewell! Farewell!"[28] The romance, slow in starting, is genuine enough, and it achieves a peak of strength some one and a half days before the ship lands; after which, the two must part, apparently forever.

These suggestions of defeated love are refined upon in the story "Your Obituary, Well Written,"[29] whose tone is comparable to the approach Henry James had to these matters. The narrator comes upon an advertisement which offers the service indicated in the story's title; and he wonders what he would like to have put in his obituary. Was there a "moment" when he rose from the drab level of his most ordinary life? He concludes that it would have been his brief friendship with the novelist, Reine Wilson, shortly before she died. The friendship had been a mutually enjoyed good talk; they had had it on only two occasions, and then the light had gone out of his experience and her life. Nevertheless, it had had a perfection worthy of being immortalized in "Your Obituary, Well Written."

Several of the stories in *Costumes By Eros* are comedies that misfire: complications without wit, or somber discussions of love on the sophomoric level. "The Necktie"[30] fumbles over an American tourist's adventures in Paris. He has tiptoed away from his ailing wife to try his charm on *les parisiennes*, but he discovers to his horror that he has come away without a necktie. He stumbles into the room of a prostitute, who offers him one of her stock of neckties (left there, apparently, by past customers) and is deeply offended that he should be interested only in them.

"A Conversation"[31] is concerned with the question of a certain woman's alleged promiscuity. "The Professor's Escape"[32] is a variant of the shipboard romance. When a professor escapes from his books and his lectures to dinner with his friends, he hears the story of one of them who had a chance meeting with a lonely woman (married, but alone) on a journey to Europe.

The professor's voice is a fatal attraction for her; her husband is a typical American businessman who has neglected her. She is "a kind of American Emma Bovary" (*Eros,* 170-71). She offers herself to him in his stateroom: "I am yours . . . irrevocably and utterly yours . . ." (175).

But, this is a horrible mistake! ". . . being a mere timid married man, unquestionably loyal and decidedly less than *moyen sensuel,* I was, to be quite frank, in a horrible funk, and could find nothing to do but look silly. . . . But I did manage, after a moment, to pull myself together—and I said, with as much gravity as I could muster, that so great a sacrifice, on her part, was out of the question, and that of course any such permanent relation between us could not for a moment be considered . . ." (175-76).

There is a parade of such women in Aiken's stories; the ratio of adulteries to happy marriages in them is rather high. These stories are not very successful; they skim the surface, or rely upon the sensational or the slightly shady to carry them through. It is not that women are less reliable in Aiken's fiction than in most, but that both men and women are uncertain of themselves, lonely, and tense over the repeated failures to achieve sexual balance. Many of the lesser stories and sketches are erotic daydreams; few achieve more than a superficial understanding of the tenuities of the relationship.

That the description of that relationship is a difficult task but that Aiken can accomplish it is testified to in the occasional successes: the novels *Great Circle, Blue Voyage* (which has other matters to discuss as well), and (perhaps in a less ambitious, a quieter, but nevertheless, a modest success) *Conversation.*[33] This last novel is likely to be lost in the discussion of Aiken's immense and varied production; and certainly, by itself, it should not have given him more of a reputation than, say, that of a Helen Howe. But it does have its merits; there are remarkable scenes with Buzzer, the five-year-old daughter (Aiken has always had a wonderful success in the portrayal of bright, imaginative children); the quarrel of husband and wife proceeds with a fine logic of disputation and a succession of irritating invitations to its renewal, until it simply collapses of its own weight, and the two adults are once more in normal, sympathetic relation; the personality clash is suitably (and not jarringly) associated with two differing views of art and Bohemia and Boston society; and its progress is counterpointed by quotations from the *Journal of the Pilgrims,* which touch gently and suggestively upon it. The Timothy Kanes are Aiken's most perfectly adjusted couple. Their differences are convincingly presented, but they do not seem to go very deep.

One of the great, uninhibited manifestations of female wiles, ingenuity, jealousy, and tension is the story, "Spider, Spider."[34] It truly compensates for the many failures in *Costumes By Eros.* It is a viciously, maliciously "right" analysis. From the very beginning the devouring female faces the wondering and submissive and bemused male. "[Gertrude] was smiling delightedly, almost voraciously; the silver scarf suited enchantingly her pale Botticelli face." She was always smiling at him in "this odd, greedy maner—showing her sharp, faultless teeth, her eyes incredibly and hungrily bright" (*Eros,* 29).

Two women compete for the hero's love: the absent May, the vividly present Gertrude. The conversation takes place in Gertrude's drawing room. She is before the fireplace, he staring at her from his chair. What about May? He thinks of marrying her, she is so simple and open and has such good taste. But don't you see, says Gertrude, this is a feminine trick; she is really a hypocrite fearful of letting herself go. ". . . She was looking back at him honestly—oh, so very honestly—her long green eyes so wide open with candor—and yet, as he always did, he couldn't help feeling that she was very deep . . ." (32). Gertrude is out to "protect" him from May. The motives are obvious, yet they seem obscure enough. It is not that she loves him but that she wishes to destroy either him or his virtuous intentions.

He is not to be persuaded—for the moment at least. "Think of considering poor May, poor ingenuous May, designing!" (33). But Gertrude will destroy her, "tear her to pieces—with that special gleaming cruelty which the sophisticated reserve for the unsophisticated" (34). She is ready to pounce upon any naïve declarations of love or trust and to turn them to her advantage. ". . . You *are* sweet, Harry. But your beautiful tenderness deserved something better . . ." (35). Gertrude continues: Don't you see, Harry, that she is out to get your money, your prestige, your social position? As she urges him to change his view of May,

She reminded him of that leopard he had seen the other day, when he had gone with his two little nieces to the Bronx. He had sat there, in his cage, so immobile, so powerful, so still, so burning with energy in his spotted brightness; and then, without the smallest change of expression, he had uttered that indescribably faraway and ethereal little cry of nostalgic yearning, his slit eyes fixed mournfully on Alison . . . (*Eros*, 35-36).

Harry, aware of what is going on, is so fascinated and numbed by the animal intelligence that is manipulating it that he willingly submits. The two women exist in hostile opposition, the one trying to destroy the image the other has painstakingly created of herself. The exchange is interrupted briefly by a silence: "He waited for her next move with an anticipation which was as pleased as it was blind . . ." (37).

Of course, the delightful memory of May is now destroyed. Gertrude accuses him of being childish for having at all believed in it. And now she offers to "save him" from her: " '. . . And if ever you feel yourself on the brink of proposing to her . . . well, then, I wish you'd propose to me. Propose to me first. . . Come to Bermuda with me. That's what I mean' " (*Eros*, 40-41). When he mutters something to the effect that it "wouldn't be fair to May," she angrily cries, "Oh, damn you and your shy arbutus!" (42).

A confusion of motives, cross-purposes, moves and countermoves now seems possible. Shouldn't he, after all, agree to Gertrude's proposal? She would "paralyze him with the narcotic, insidious poison of her love . . ." (43). Then, ". . . He was going to embrace her—he was going to give himself up. And May, stooping for arbutus in the wood, became remote, was swept off into the ultimate, into the infinite, into the forgotten. May was at last definitely lost—May was dead . . ." (*Eros*, 45).

In the end, he goes quietly. The "betrayal and the agony" are over. Gertrude has won. "And then he felt himself beginning to smile; while with his finger and thumb, he gently tweaked a tiny golden watch-spring of hair which curled against the nape of the white neck" (46). He has submitted, after all, knowingly, and from fascination with the process of the seduction. The lovely May is left behind, as are his doubts and hesitations about what he should do. He is, in short, caught in the spider's web, but a more knowing fly there never was.

"Spider, Spider" distinguishes itself by being relentlessly and wholly and quite unpretentiously itself. It is also a shrewd analysis of the psychological parry and thrust of the love game. A sophisticated comedy of love-manners, it escapes the banalities of quick, easy satire (of "The Necktie," for example) as well as the portentous, half-alive attempts to invest the relationship with "meaning." It is by no means all that can be said of the relationship, but it is sufficient unto its needs; and it quite superbly, self-sufficiently holds within its limits.

VI

There are many reasons for considering *Blue Voyage*[35] a culmination. It is not necessarily Aiken's best novel, for there are too many echoes in it of contemporary masters and contemporary ideas. But in the light of Aiken's attempts to prove, to explain, and to establish himself before his public, it is a most important work. There is some suspicion that Aiken, having failed to make himself "clear" in his poetry—or at least to make himself known—turned to the novel in the hope of capturing an audience for himself and for his poetry. For he is, after all, a poet first; he is a novelist and a writer of short stories "also," "as well."

Houston Peterson (*Melody*, 231-60) describes the long way Aiken took to completing *Blue Voyage*. His first collection of short stories appeared in 1925, three years after he had begun writing the novel. And he may have begun it because of the remarkable incentive of James Joyce's *Ulysses,* published by Shakespeare and Company in Paris in 1922, for Aiken began *Blue Voyage* in the winter of 1922-23, at Winchelsea, England, where he had set up his home; then, when he moved to Rye—near where Henry James had lived—he continued it, writing chapters II, III, and IV in the winter of 1924-25. In January of 1926, he wrote chapters V and VI in America, and finished it the next summer. The information is useful only to suggest the hesitations Aiken seems to have felt over it; he was a poet, after all, and secondly a critic of poetry. Surely the new fiction offered a challenge similar to that of poetry?

Whatever the incentives for writing it, *Blue Voyage* is a genuine testimony of the artist's fictional *"apologia pro specie sua."* All of the themes that had been haunting him in his poetry are here. William Demarest is Senlin, Festus, Punch; he is in mid-ocean, in "Second Class," in a state of nerves and in a state of expectation. The scene is itself in an almost perfect frame for his deliberations. In Second Class, he looks up the ladder to an inaccessible First Class, where lives (at first unknown to him) the inaccessible First Class love, Cynthia. Down there, in the "hold," are other, easier loves, and much aimless, frantic talk; further down, in the recesses of his unconscious, are the rationalizations and debates and defenses of his art and his love.

The image of the voyage has been discussed so often that its significance for Aiken should be obvious. Demarest is traveling to England, ostensibly to try out one of his plays, apparently to seek out Cynthia, actually to discover himself. The implications of the sea's immensities are rich and various. Men and women "open themselves" to each other on a sea voyage; it is a time of frank and easy discussion. The general fright over being together and yet so menacingly isolated, so "close to the infinite" also uneasily draws them together. But Demarest is on a voyage for special reasons. He is quite thoroughly at odds with himself, a timid, proud man, who must somehow pull his ego into the light of day.

Immediately, a number of polarities become obvious. The dread purity of his Cynthia (whom he loves with a pure, romantic, nervous drive) is posed in contrast with the accommodating widow, Faubion: as the novel progresses, Cynthia rejects him; as it ends, Faubion taps at his cabin door. There is the figure of Smith, who after thirty years of selling sheet music in New Orleans is going home to England—to die. He, as the shipboard "father" to Dedalus-Demarest "son," offers his strangely cliché-ridden, somewhat obscene, altogether lonely "advice" to the young man, who on his own conceives himself a master of wit but at the same time is altogether unsure of his gift.

There is another relationship, that of Demarest to Silberstein, who is going to England to introduce American chewing gum to the natives and who meanwhile comes down to Second Class to escape the boredom of the First. Silberstein is *the* wise old man; he becomes an amateur psychoanalyst, or at least listens in the manner of the Jewish confidant to Demarest's cries of distress. Superintending all of these is the contrast of the vast immensities of the sea with the enforced intimacies of close living in cabin, dining room, and lounge: a scramble of living, a symbol of death and infinity.

Demarest is himself self-consciously aware of depths and layers of consciousness. He has become acquainted with psychoanalysis, and he knows ". . . Everybody of course, was like this —depth beyond depth, a universe chorally singing, incalculable, obeying tremendous laws, chemical or divine, of which it was able to give its own consciousness not the faintest inkling . . ." (*Voyage*, 15). Like the figures in Aiken's "Symphonies," Demarest is aware of the multitudinous worlds and microcosms of self: "A steaming universe of germ-cells, a maelstrom of animal forces, of which he himself, his personality, was only the collective gleam . . ." (16).

Mostly, his "inferiority" (he is at a party at which he is not wanted; he is an intruder) and his sense of his own misery disturb him. He half believes—or, would like to believe—that he is bearing in his art the burden of all human misery, but he cannot ever quite bring himself to accept the role of Christ that that would suggest.

In any case, the passengers, on the second day (always the crucial day) of the voyage, are extraordinarily conscious of one another—probing and sizing each other up, making plans, and shuffling and rearranging egos. ". . . the yearning confusion of friendliness, curiosity, loneliness, and love, which made them all puppets and set them bowing and nodding at one another . . ." (*Voyage*, 33). Smith is above all the epitome of "the tragic helplessness of the human": on his way to a small town in England, where he is sure no one will remember him, in what Demarest calls "an unconscious desire for death, for the mother . . ." (51-52). His situation makes the friendliness of the widow Faubion especially grotesque. Demarest has a fantastic vision of Faubion's approaching Smith in his coffin: ". . . And lo, Smith lived; the coffin glowed about him, an incandescent chrysalis, burning translucently, within which lay Smith, gleaming and waxing; . . . with fiery veins and God-like nimbus, sprang up rejoicing, naked and blazing, a leafy vine of gold rapidly growing all over his body and burning off as it grew . . ." (*Voyage*, 59).[36]

This fantasy is of course related to Demarest's confusion over the choice of Dionysus or Apollo. He is at once in his imagination both the shy, timid suitor of the exquisite Cynthia and the sly seducer of every other woman on the boat. But his sexual energies are diverted into words: he will seduce the world through art, then save it from its fate. ". . . Love (he had been taught) was sensuality, sensuality was evil, evil was prohibited but delicious: the catechism of the vacant lot. But how, then, had beauty come in? How had it so managed to complicate itself with evil and sensuality and the danks and darks of sex?—" (101). The widow Faubion, for example, was "a vigorous synthesis" of all his past loves; yet he spurned her and sought after Cynthia, who burned with a cold light indeed.

The shocking discovery is made early enough. Cynthia *is* aboard and is going to England (he had supposed he was going to England to find her). When Demarest—on a forbidden walk about the upper deck—encounters her, she tells him she is to be married. He is the "sneaking interloper," beneath her class, now out of all hope of reaching her person.

That night he lies on his cabin bed, his lively imagination fighting sleep, his conscience and resentment making a shambles of reason. The result is a tortured confusion of subconscious images mingled with deceptively rational discourses on love, art, perfidy, and misery. The thought is trained at Cynthia, a grotesquely self-defensive effort to rid his mind of her engagement to be married: ". . . My face is the face of one grown gently wise with suffering—ah, with what years of untold suffering! I have been misunderstood,—I have blundered,—I have sinned,—Oh, I have sinned; but I have paid the price . . ." (*Voyage,* 123).

Demarest's mind wanders vagrantly over many psychic extremes: vengeance, inferiority, misery, rationalization, self-crucifixion: "I am wise, I am weak, I am persecuted; . . ." (129). What underlies all of the torment is the clash of the two loves —sacred and profane, Cynthia and Faubion, seduction and the love ethereal. He grovels before Cynthia in his mind's abasement, protesting innocence, or at least promising to pretend to it if she will still have (135). Then, the fantasy turns to the thought of his shedding blood for God's sake and for man's. His two drops of blood fall in heaven, "like thunder claps. The angels fly up like doves. God, asleep, has a dream . . ." (140). Demarest has become Christ, suffering (in his confusion) the misery of the human race, which is only his own misery enlarged.

The interior monologue fastens upon its root-source: Demarest is "a verbalist . . . a tinkling symbolist. I am the founder and leader of a new school of literature—the Emblemists . . ." (156). Here again, his appeal (partly to the absent Cynthia, partly to himself) is a melange of boasting and cringing: he is a Greenwich Village poet, "slightly eccentric, but really quite commonplace . . ." (157); he is Maxwell Bodenheim, showing his poems to people on trains, in restaurants, on park benches; he is "that immoral and hypocritical *fin de siècle* Jesus" (158).

The half-conscious dialogue with Cynthia continues into the night and morning: Demarest "making" claims and boasts that are contrary to his real nature, Cynthia trilling her delight, or being shocked. Then he begins a monologue on the relationship of suffering to art. "But there's no concealing the suffering it has brought, that frightful and inescapable and unwearying consciousness of the unattainable. The soul aching every moment, every hour, with sharp brief paroxysms of intenser pain: the eyes closing in vain, sleep vainly invited . . ." (*Voyage*, 166-67).

The suffering is mixed with his sense of erotic deprivation, until—like Bloom in *Ulysses*—Demarest undergoes trial for "erotomania . . . Pity me, Cynthia! . . ." (172). He is in Hell, Cynthia in Paradise; but he is not Dante and will not reach his Beatrice. Out of despair, he turns to the Christ image. He will do good to all on board, by crucifying his SELF, so that "my personality will cease" (189).

The long, tortuous journey through and around his psychic hurt ceases. Demarest, on deck once more the next day, discusses with Silberstein (the chewing-gum merchant) the psychology of the artist—a familiar argument encountered in several of Aiken's critical essays.[37] We are all of us frustrated, starved, for love, or praise, or power, and "our entire characters are moulded by these thwarted longings . . ." (214). And "'. . . we can see ourselves thus with a profound narcissistic compassion, ourselves godlike in stature and power, going down to a defeat which lends us an added glory . . . Art is therefore functionally exaggerative . . .'" (*Voyage*, 214).

It is interesting to see this discourse with Silberstein in the light of Stephen Dedalus' discussions with Lynch and with Cranly in Joyce's *A Portrait of the Artist as a Young Man*. There are some parallels, but both the character of the declaration and the motives for it are radically different. Demarest is rebelling against no one; he is, in fact, falling back upon theory in the interests of rationalizing his failure to rebel.

Since Dedalus was to rebel against the spirit of the Catholic faith but not against its forms, he was able to formulate a theory of art that has been the wonder of critics and scholars since. Further, for him art was substantive; for Demarest it is affectively true, and *only* affectively true. The success of a work of art, he says to Silberstein, depends on whether it gives the reader an illusion, "if it convinces him, and, in convincing him, adds something to his experience both in range and coherence, both in command of feeling and command of expression . . ." (*Voyage*, 215).

Demarest's remarks become more and more badly tangled in his own psychological wound as he proceeds. Why not, he says, write the great play, whose hero is a modern type of Christ? But, better than that, who not *act out* the Christ, rather than write Him into a play? Why not go the last step to the ultimate sacrifice—give up writing, give up forcing one's ego on others? He does not himself suggest "sublimation," but the thought comes later to him when, in an imaginary conversation with a psychoanalyst, he is advised to resort to it (*Voyage*, 240).

Chapter V is a fantasy constructed from the notion of "sublimation." All of Demarest's acquaintances on board ship are fashioned into a kind of inverted "Circe" scene. Demarest himself says: "We accept everything. We deny nothing. We are, in fact, imagination: not completely, for then we should be God; but almost completely. Perhaps, in time, our imagination *will* be complete" (*Voyage*, 250). But this essay in harmony does not endure; it is bound to break down, in view of Demarest's psychological economy. As he had in the monologue of the previous evening, he again debases himself, this time in the form of a mock trial: his "impurial highness" is cast down, and Cynthia is transformed "for all time, into a stained-glass widow" (264, 266).

The novel concludes as Demarest resorts to two kinds of therapy: letters to Cynthia (none of them sent, one of them not written); and the widow Faubion. In the letters, he finds himself alternating between essays in self-pride and exercises in denigration. Gradually, the incentive for composing them seems to diminish, until the fifth letter has only one phrase, and the sixth is blank. He continues to "chew away" at his own misery until there is none left.

As for the second kind of therapy, there is no guarantee that it will have a lasting effect, and no assurance that it isn't Demarest "taking second best." In any case, Faubion, who has visited several cabins on the voyage, now taps questioningly on the door of his. Demarest, who has been wondering if Cynthia was yet asleep, responds to the tap, half expecting or hoping that it is Cynthia; he stands watching the door softly open and Faubion enter (*Voyage*, 318).

However difficult it may be to assess the value of *Blue Voyage*, it is certain that it should no longer simply be considered an "experiment in the stream-of-consciousness novel," nor merely compared (to its disadvantage) with *Ulysses*.[38] Its values ought rather to be considered in terms of its place in Aiken's writings. The primary consideration of it might be devoted to its success as a Portrait of the Artist as a Middle-Aged Man. As such, *Blue Voyage* scintillates at times, is dull at others. It cleverly imitates and quite adequately defines the habits of a variety of human types, but at times drops them in the interests of "ideas" —or, rather, of the artist's defense of himself, which ranges from self-derogation to exaltation to theoretic explanations of his "cause" (or why and how he is as he is). The style is admirably clever and hopelessly gauche; puns do not last, even when they are intended as evidence in a characterization. On the other hand, Demarest's interior monologue is for the most part expertly done. It does not have, however, the sense of "ringing tone" that the dreams of Andy Cather have in *Great Circle*.

Perhaps the one fault that keeps *Blue Voyage* from being more than the very interesting, often intelligent and at times brilliant work that it is, is that the parts do not cohere meaningfully except as they relate to Demarest's plight; and his situation is not sufficient to justify the display of technical and experimental skills. There is a point at which the "literariness" of *Blue Voyage* ceases to be interesting, simply because Demarest is insufficiently interesting. This we cannot say about *Ulysses*, for Demarest's counterpart in it is not by any means the center and his brilliantly clever excursions into the affairs of the mind are taken for what they are; which is to say that Joyce's irony saves *Ulysses*, at points where Aiken's fails *Blue Voyage*.

The fact also remains that Aiken's sense of character—of narrator, hero, villain, victim—is not wholly adequate. Andy Cather's distressful maneuverings around his unconscious memory are admirably coherent, but beyond the crisis that has impelled him, Cather is not exceptionally important as a person. Demarest is more versatile and has more "sides"; yet we actually know less about him than we do of Cather. And this not from lack of information, but because the "central situation" is simply not convincingly given.

What, after all, do we know of Cynthia, that we should be so much concerned with her? For that matter, what does Demarest know of her? And isn't it true that the central facts of Demarest's agony are so quickly grasped and so easily dismissed as to make much of the elaboration an extravagant (often a brilliant) repetition of the obvious?

In any case, *Blue Voyage* seems to me to have receded more and more from its prominent position of 1927 (when it was considered an "experimental novel"), leaving it to be examined in the light of *what* it says, despite the often exhilarating sense of its having said it cleverly, absorbingly, often superbly. If we are to have an artist as hero, his role as artist should meaningfully relate to a decision he has made as person. This decision Demarest does not make, and the theorizing seems, therefore, to diminish his personality instead of enhancing and strengthening it. The strength of his agony comes neither from Cynthia (who is not realized) nor from himself; it lies merely in the words and images used to describe it. As a consequence, instead of looking into the center of a tragically tortured sensitivity, we are engaged too much in marking and translating formulas from the images offered as evidence of a very limited character.

CHAPTER *3*

The Poetry:
The Man of Many Devices

I

EVEN from a point some forty-eight years after his first publication, it is difficult to evaluate a man's poetry when there
is such a rich profusion of it. Since 1914 (the year of *Earth
Triumphant*), Conrad Aiken has published a total of twenty-
nine volumes of poems: these include the *Selected Poems* of
1929 (for which, in 1930, he received the Pulitzer Prize), the
Collected Poems of 1953, and the recent edition of *Selected
Poems* (1961). Certain other volumes are reprintings or rear-
rangements of poems previously published. The 1949 publication of *The Divine Pilgrim* by the University of Georgia Press
is an example: in it all of the "Symphonies," from the *Charnel
Rose* to "Changing Mind," are reordered, some of them much
revised, and equipped with prefaces and explanations. But the
majority of the volumes are fresh, new, original poems, which
add steadily to the reputation of the poet.

How do we "place" Aiken as a poet? Henry Wells calls him
"a direct heir of the romantic movement," and he cites Poe,
Keats, and others by way of evidence.[1] Julian Symons says, "His
poetry is that of a graceful and gentle hedonist expressing rather
than interpreting or valuing the flux of modern life."[2] R. P.
Blackmur invokes Wallace Stevens, for comparison with the
poet of *Preludes for Memnon* and *Time in the Rock*: ". . . Each
is deeply concerned with the interminable labor and single solace
of the imagination. . . . And each knows that imagination has
an end, and how, and why, and where. . . . And each, finally,
knows by what means the imagination is to be resurrected. . . ."[3]

But more must be said of this relation; and Blackmur, one of a handful of "independent," sympathetic readers of Aiken's poetry, says it. Aiken is more "the traditional poet" than is Stevens: "He writes with the habit and the assurance of the traditional poet; his preludes, as he masters them, became, like the Elizabethan sonnet or the heroic couplet, a definite and predictable form of thinking; and his underlying meaning flows from the hidden predispositions of his time" (*The Expense of Greatness*, 222).

The problem of assessing Aiken as poet is one of noting his growth. As is the case of any substantial poet, there are several stages in this growth. In the beginning, there are juvenilia, in which the sources imitated are spoiled by the imitation. There is a time of acceleration, in which ideas and forms occur in such abundance that the poetry can only occasionally take proper advantage of them. This is followed by an attempt to formulate independent modes and philosophies; in Aiken's case, it is the parallels of music, of thematic structures and rhythms. Rufus Blanshard, Aiken's best critic, explains this phase of his development: "Repetition in the symphonies is Aiken's poetic equivalent of musical restatement. Sometimes a whole section reappears as a reprise. . . More often it is a selective repetition, a variation. . . ."[4]

Aiken moves beyond the "symphonies." The years from 1925 to 1931 are years of consolidation and refinement. The scope of the individual poems diminishes, and the individual lines and forms submit to close and profitable scrutiny. The Preludes of 1931 and 1936, which most critics who are at all willing to give Aiken a fair reading have applauded, are a culmination as well as a new direction. They are followed by "occasional" volumes, some of them utilizing the methods of the Preludes; others, an experiment in an independent mode or a revision of an old one; still others, "compilations" of the good and the ordinary. Looking back upon almost a half century of Aiken's practice, we may say that the time of the Preludes still remains the "time of genius."

A few other preliminary remarks need to be made. One is that Aiken is an extraordinarily gifted poet. The terms "profligate genius," "versatility," and "great richness and variety" come to mind. From the beginning his poems have demonstrated not only an exceptional, a "natural," sense of word, line, elementary form but also a great sensitivity to the work of his contemporaries and his tradition. (This is responsible as well for making him the good critic he is.)

I should add to these qualities a restless desire to experiment, to seek out new ways and means of expanding the structure of his poems and of bringing particular insights within the range of new perceptive orders. As a critic, he was sensitive from the beginning to both the attractions and the risks of new, experimental modes. But he was too much the gifted traditionalist to go to extremes of non-classical, "modern" forms. Rather, his development has been toward a modern restatement of traditional manners.

We may also ask: what has he been saying all this while? Joseph Warren Beach offers the extreme answer: Aiken is preoccupied with the "moral terror" of modern life, "the deathlike emptiness of the living experience itself, and all that lies about it . . ." (*Obsessive Images*, 63). Other critics have been more moderate in their assessment of Aiken's trial "definitions": he is the "graceful hedonist," the "restless explorer," the man seeking imaginative order. Aiken has himself used the term "consciousness" as the key word. In *Ushant*, he comes back again and again to it; in his prefatory statements about the "Symphonies," it is obvious that a "consciousness" is involved in each case; and in his critical reviews, the word occurs in a variety of contexts. Aiken intends the word to have both a substantive value and an activist meaning. It is "self-knowledge," but it has also a creative impact on the objects of knowledge. The poet actively creates as he comes to know.

The process is reiterative. The poietic function is to move forward into a "blankness," a chaos of matter, to impose an order upon it or find one in it, then to "double back" upon itself. This action leads to a steady enhancement of the shaping power of consciousness. There are also emotional values, or qualities; these are "metaphysical" or "ontological," as opposed to "moral." The observer of Aiken's poems (Senlin, Festus, the "I" of "Changing Mind," or, simply, the poet who superintends the creative act) *sees* values in the universe, which he brings forth from it; his instrument is the word, the "Word made word," words in many formal combinations and with many echoes and overtones.

In *Ushant,* he speaks of Henry Adams having "predicted that the early years of the twentieth century would witness the flowering of an ultimate phase . . . in man's thinking, a final brilliance of consciousness, as of the world itself coming to self-knowledge. . . ." He also describes the poet as a "religious" man, in the sense that he is "a poietic shaper of his own destiny, through self-knowledge and love . . ." (*Ushant,* 219-20). Blanshard has rightly pointed to these remarks as representing a reversal of the Elizabethan view. There is no "divine ordering" in Aiken's view; his is the ordering and succession of images and sensations, and of "poetic acts" and "imaginative maneuvers" undertaken with the privileges and risks of a secular and existential point of view.

These remarks help to explain why Aiken's poetry so often seems to "repeat itself"; why it appears to return again and again to the same issues. Much the same may be said of Stevens' poetry, except that there is often a greater certainty of ideational progress in it. It is, in either case, a dialectic of sorts, moving in and out of the phenomenal world in the hope of bringing definition to it.

The two terms that emerge as strongest from these remarks are "consciousness" and "definition." They are the keystones of Aiken's theoretics. Consciousness itself comprehends a wide range of poetic resource; it is as much a reference to the "subconscious" or unconscious wells of imagery as it is a conventional term, descriptive of the active mind.[5] The term "definition" has several variations on the way to Aiken's later use of it. At times it seems that we need to substitute a less clarifying term for it: improvisation of experience, for example; or the dramatization of query and dilemma. It occasionally means what John Crowe Ransom does by the "ontological values" of the poetic object: that is, the strength and power of the word, not only to define but to identify metaphysical meaning; so that the imagination moves on successive levels of comprehension.

Aiken does not go the full way with Ransom; it is perhaps not because he does not see the necessity, but rather because he suspects a risk in going too far beyond the word. Neither of the terms, *consciousness* and *definition,* can be said to remain static. Aiken subjects both to incessant "public" alteration (in the sense that a published poem is a "public" performance). The rapidity and frequency of his improvisations have caused many a critic to say, with Allen Tate, that Aiken has too many intellectual formulas "that are not sharply differentiated and brought to heel by the imagination," and to insist that "the logical and the musical forms require different spans of attention. . . ."[6]

Critics offer a common complaint about the bewildering and apparently formless and erratic richness of his gift. J. G. Southworth defines this "cry of 'Enough'" as well as any when he suggests that, instead of the "significant form of a Haydn or Mozart symphony he gives us something more nearly akin to the diffuse symphonies of Bruckner and Mahler."[7] The reader may decide for himself if the "profligacy of effect" is a mark of genius or the result of a failure of control, or perhaps both.

II

It would be manifestly unwise to decide this question from a reading of Aiken's earliest poetry, especially since he has dismissed all of it from the *Collected Poems.* The poems he wrote while he was a student at Harvard (1907-12) and a big man in the offices of the *Advocate* were outpourings of an adolescent's interests in his immediate past as well as blank imitations of the poets he was reading in the classroom and out. Houston Peterson, who marks Aiken's literary beginnings much earlier, speaks of his experiences as a boy in New Bedford, especially the "glassed-in cupola (that miniature light-house of New Bedford homes), where he read and dreamed and looked down on the glamorous harbors, ferrys, tugboats, fishing smacks and the shining mast of a whaling vessel, about to go out on its last adventure" (*Melody,* 28). Even earlier, perhaps at the age of nine, he wrote his first poem, "Lex Talionis," preserved by Peterson (*Melody,* 24-25).

Rufus Blanshard speaks of a long narrative poem that Aiken wrote in 1911 at Harvard: *The Clerk's Journal: Being the Diary of a Queer Man.*

. . . Here are the gaucheries of diction and taste one might expect, and the sentimentality of subject insufficiently disguised by irony. But already Aiken was experimenting in the direction of the later symphonies and the serial poems, already mixing the quotidian and the "poetic," already charting a mind's successive moods with repetition and contrast of "emotion-masses" (as he later called them) . . . ("Pilgrim's Progress," 136).

"Le Penseur" (*Advocate Anthology,* 119-21)[9] describes the creation of a statue that acquires consciousness and cries out against the pain of being alone. The statue's complaint is the conventional, youthful adaptation without any original embellishments of the romantic notion of "unheard beauties." "Why do you hew me out of marble, Man?" he speaks, and he goes on, to talk of his long, peaceful sleep, before "Some meddling god . . . / . . . bids me stir." The consciousness of a world accustomed to "break, to snare, to kill, to overcome—" is a painful one; and he begs the sculptor to lull him with "a sweeter song," so that he may gain "Once more the sleep of marble; lose once more / The world and Thee and all unhappiness" (*Advocate Anthology,* 121).

"Le Reveur"[10] is a variant of the same notion. A sculptor yearns to work a miracle: he will reshape "this shaggy brute" of man into a god. The conventionally romantic idea of the artist's power is here put down in a mechanical echo of Browning's monologues.

> Already do I feel my nostrils flare
> In ecstasy of sensuous bliss,—I know
> Already how my breath will sear my lips,

Despite the dull glowering look he gives his master, the latter is inspired to go on, to make from rock the perfect man.

> O, I will make him luminous with soul,
> This starless creature pale with dreams of stars. . . .
> What if it pain him, or he long to sleep?
> Hot is the impulse, now—bring me the chisel!
>
> (122, 123)

"To a Head in Marble" (*Advocate Anthology,* 123-26)[11] is another variant of the same theme. In it the artist envies the very lack of the consciousness he has, in the other poems, yearned to give to his statues. The "virgin head," "Maiden of marble,—charmed,—immutable!" enjoys an inestimable advantage over her creator: "I too would turn to stone, and leave behind / Earth's griefs that open wide our eyes, earth's joys that blinds" (124). Art here conveys immortality, which the artist, who is made of ordinary clay, cannot himself enjoy. To it he nevertheless aspires, so that winds and snows and seasonal change need not afflict him. "This night will pass, its storm remembered not; / To-morrow dawns, this darkness is forgot" (126).

This verse has less than ordinary value for the student of Aiken's poetry. There is some advantage in noting the beginning of a metrical skill, especially in the complicated pattern of the third poem's ten-line stanzas. The conventional and superficial idea of the two worlds of a fixed "beauty" and of a mortal man is one that will persist in Aiken's verse, though with much more subtle elaboration than is seen here. The melancholy and sentimental cry of the pain of participation in human affairs is to lead shortly to a frequently iterated complaint that beauty is always threatened by evil and decay.

The formation of an "esthétique de mal" is far away. Ultimately, of course, Aiken will abandon the superficial notion of the separation of matter into a "hard core" immortal substance and an unhappy impermanence. There is no promise in these early poems of the subtlety which Aiken was eventually to bring to his conception of the consciousness and its relationship to matter. If we speculate upon the date (1910-11), however, and consider the state of aesthetic "propriety" of the time—not yet affected by a "new poetry" that was just beginning—then the "achievements" of the *Advocate* verse are more acceptable; and we are left with speculations concerning the very imperfect signs of a poetic gift.

III

From his first volume of poetry, *Earth Triumphant and Other Tales in Verse*,[12] Aiken reprinted nothing, either in the *Selected Poems* of 1929 or in *The Collected Poems* of 1953. There seemed to be nothing salvageable. Aiken was twenty-five years old when the volume appeared. He was actually on the edge of his first "push" of experimental and independent verse; but there is little here to suggest that he was. Nor is there a glimmer of suspicion that Eliot was beginning to publish the poems that were featured in *Prufrock and Other Observations,* or that Ezra Pound was well launched, with several volumes of poetry and associations with two or three magazines of the "new poetry" and prose. The Imagist "manifesto" of 1912 finds no echo in

Earth Triumphant. Indeed, the poetry in it is lavishly and richly amateurish, a riot of "colour" in the least desirable sense of that term, and an elaborate and romantic display of traditional and romantic rhyme and rhythm patterns.

Aiken offers a disclaiming foreword, in which he claims some rights of separation from the influence of John Masefield, with which he correctly predicts he will be charged.

> . . . I feel compelled to say here, in view of the fact that I am certain to be called an imitator of Masefield, that before I had ever heard of Masefield I was experimenting with narrative poems of modern daily life. In one case I had even employed the octosyllabic couplet (used so successfully in "The Everlasting Mercy") to tell the love-story of an ordinary clerk (*Earth Triumphant,* vii).[13]

The influence of Masefield is nevertheless, and avowedly, pervasive; and there were to be several complimentary references to him in the critical essays of the next years (*Scepticisms,* 1919). Although a temporary indebtedness, it was damaging to the verse of *Earth Triumphant* and to that of the years following; for even a superficial glance will prove that Masefield's love of obvious rhythms, of "dead-end" rhyme sounds, and of the bravado of verse narrative finds a continuous echo. The jingling upsets the nerves, distracts the attention, causes the reader to lose the values the poetry might have given him. More than that, the poetry is sententious, clumsily and unnaturally formal, and blunted at the idea's edge. Aiken would much rather cross a street than turn a corner. The value of idea in *Earth Triumphant* is scarcely much higher than that of the *Advocate* poems. The poet is still in his long sleep.

The long title poem (pp. 1-68) is a mélange of romantic poses and attitudes. The hero as youth has, by candlelight, "Ere his own life was yet begun," exhausted "Each creed, each weird philosophy, / And reached at last satiety" (4). Forswearing art, he decides to go directly to nature, and first experiments with sin: the gayly lighted streets, where walked the girls,

> Who held their bodies but as bread,
> As broken bread, not more divine,
> And no more precious blood than wine.
>
> (6)

There is a "metaphysical pleasantry" in the idea of prostitutes offering their bodies as Christ had His that is not too far from what Aiken was to develop in later poems: that is, that the most affecting religious testimony in nature is the offering of sex and the real struggle lies in its having no adequate guarantee of immortality.

There is an easy octosyllabic step from "bodies" to one body, and then to his beloved's arms, of which he has "imperious need" (12). Love-making is now purposeful, not just a means of fleeing a lifeless study.

> But something, some dim restlessness,
> Of which he scarce had consciousness,
> The subtle impulse that in spring
> Makes daisies grow and thrushes sing,
> Left him discontent with this,—
> To talk of her, forego her kiss.
>
> (15)

It is, of course, the poem's crisis. He will hope that the intensity of his love for her will adequately replace, or will even yield, immortality. But this it cannot do; for the irony of love is that it too must yield to death.

> Still she lay silent, like one dead . . .
> At times, his grief was passionate
> And he cried out, importunate;
>
> (30-31)

Nothing will return her to life. He begs her, passionately, to rise from death, but she does not respond. He begins therefore a time of passionate refusal. The earth, so eloquently convincing before, now mocks him with its "soulless" decay. "An absence of all loveliness, / Came down upon his heart like rain" (39).

Slowly, earth triumphs over his loss and pain, and he concedes that her death may after all be a "return to earth," and that perhaps the brilliance of nature is herself restored to him.

> And then he felt new life in him
> Like flowers of red surge up and swim
> Through all his blood; and all earth moved
> With life of her whom he had loved,
> Till she was earth and earth was she,

> She was this snow, this brook, this tree . . .
> And joy rose up in him, and song,
> As buoyantly he walked along:
>
> (61)

What strikes one immediately in this poem is its great ease and simplicity, both of idea and execution. The youth moves quickly from diagnostics to action to pain to despair to cure. Partly this speed is the result of the monotonous acceleration of the form. Octosyllabic couplets require a certain pungency of thought; the words should at least occasionally twist and gnarl and lie in the way of metrical progress; or the culmination of rhyme should in itself encourage a pause. These things do not happen in "Earth Triumphant." But mostly the fault lies in the absence of intellectual hardness. There is neither the reward of plurisignative language nor any dramatic sharpness. We do not believe either in the young man or in his love, so we care little about what happens to them, or about the means he uses to resolve his difficulties and to heal his wound.

There are some Scollay Square dynamics in "Youth," the next long poem of the volume (*Earth Triumphant*, 69-131); that is, a patois sometimes replaces the thee-thou refrain. But this is rather like saying "Hully Gee!" instead of "Alas, Alack." The form is more intricate; the eight-line stanzas rhyming *ababbbcc* would seem designed to slow down the reading; but it gallops nevertheless.

At the same time Aiken published *Earth Triumphant*, and before it, E. A. Robinson was putting variant eight-line stanzas to a much more successful use. The difference lies not in formal excellence (though even in this Robinson is quite superior), but in *what* the lines are saying. Robinson used the form to say much in a short space, to develop that statement shrewdly; and he left much unsaid that would only get in the way of the saying. "Youth" is, however, almost barren of ideas and with a pressure so light that we may almost say it has no intensity at all.

The poem begins with an appeal to mother earth to reveal her secrets, to give justice to those who seek it, "Or happiness, maybe; . . ." (71); and it proceeds to narrate the life of one of earth's creatures. At first eloquently proud of his strength, health, courage, "Crushing the sea, his body all one song" (73), the youth exults in his freedom: "A lust for life, for power, a hot clear passion / All earth unto his own heart's peace to fashion . . ." (78).

He is aware of his "differences" from the bickering, whimpering men, and quits his job, "not caring what came after." He joins a gang, "whose work was crime" (86). Women, drunk with lust for him, yearn to strip "and leave bright bodies bare . . ." (94). But the life palls quickly; the youth flees the city (having first killed a jealous lover) into the mountains in search of earth, the strong and urgent mother; for "Youth was a knife, he would not let it rust!— / But cut with it, cut merciless to the core . . ." (106).

Tenderness comes to his soul, in the person of Jane, the farmer's daughter, "Quiet and calm, sweet spirit of this place" (113). The poem closes on this exultant note:

> He closed his eyes and knew now what life meant;
> (123)

> . . . .

> Youth rose, youth fell; she smiled to sun, danced on,
> Smiling the same smile, dancing, dawn to dawn.
> (131)

"Romance" (*Earth Triumphant*, 132-66) is the first of Aiken's many shipboard adventures in verse and prose. Again we find the easy encounter of youth, the dropping of shyness, the progress of love. In it, however, the young man proves unfaithful to the occasion, and this provides the occasion for a simple ironic thrust.

> O youth, O music, O sweet wizardry
> Of young love sung like fire through beating veins!
> (157)

But as it turns out, he'd not really meant to love her, except in a love game.

The rest of the poems are scarcely above the level of "Romance." "Earth Tedium" (*Earth Triumphant*, 167-82) is a lesser version of the title poem. "Sophistication" (185-95) describes a man who has strayed too far from "the warm sunrise of his birth" (195) and is, therefore, sickened of life:

That life is sick that questions life;
And this he knew, but knew too late,
For he had passed through wisdom's gate
And seen of what stuff life is made,—
The thin web woven out of dust,

(189)

In "Laughter (Youth Speaks to His Own Old Age)" (196-202), the young man sees himself as old, weak, "drooling wisdom day by day" (197). There are additional echoes of the first two long poems: "Youth Imperturbable" (203-6), in which his confidence in his strength remains undiminished; and "Youth Penetrant" (207-9), in which he laughs at age and death. In the two concluding poems, Aiken addresses himself to the poets themselves: poets must find their poetry in life, must leave the study and immerse themselves in life ("Parasitics: To Certain Poets," 210-15); and the modern poet has an especially hard time:

Hirelings are we of the time.
God pity us! For we must seek
In city filth, in streets that reek
Dark inspiration for our rhyme.
("Dilemma," 217)

A less promising first volume can scarcely be imagined. There is a certain facility; in fact, the metrical and formal dexterity and quickness recommend the volume. Sixty-eight pages of octosyllabic heroics are in themselves a kind of achievement. It is undoubtedly true that this surface skill encouraged Aiken to experiment with the "symphonic form" later. But whatever effect that form had on his choice, the rhetoric seems remarkably empty and monotonous and awkward. We have become so used to weighing poetic values closely that the experience of reading *Earth Triumphant* is too much like walking in syrup to be comfortable.

IV

Turns and Movies[14] is a very different kind of work. Perhaps the superior effectiveness of these poems comes from their having been dramatically centered, instead of being victimized by a quick narrative sweep. We have a sense of genuine, legiti-

mate feelings in these statements by vaudevillians and circus-
men.

The volume is imitative still. Houston Peterson speaks of the
three years (1913-16) when Aiken was writing these poems;
he "haunted the Orpheum vaudeville theater in Boston, where
beauty and sordidness, ignorance and art gave him their weekly
summary of the world . . ." (*Melody*, 36). It was the time also
when Edgar Lee Masters was writing the poems that went into
The Spoon River Anthology (1915), and these poems (which
appeared in *Reedy's Mirror, Poetry*, and elsewhere) must have
directed Aiken in the form his title poems were to take. Aiken
explained his restoring these to *Collected Poems* (they had been
omitted from *Selected Poems*) on the grounds that, "though
immature and uneven [they seem to me] to have at least a
crude vitality" ("Preface" to *CP*). This they do have, and perhaps
a little more.

The fifteen psychological sketches look inside the minds of
performing artists on the vaudeville stage.

> He mimics wooing her, without a sound,
> Flatters her with a smoothly smiled caress.
> He fears that she will some day queer his act;
> Feeling her anger. He will quit her soon.
> He nods for faster music. He will contract
> Another partner, under another moon.
> ("Rose and Murray," *CP*, 3)

The actor of "The Apollo Trio" (4-5) despises his lot:

> What he hates
> Is traveling with these damned degenerates,
> Tight-trousered, scented, both with women's hips,
> With penciled eyes, and lean vermilioned lips.

For the most part, the performers have a deep hatred, or
jealousy, for each other. The grace of their movements hides a
variety of strong emotions: "She looks down on him with a look
of hatred, / And wishes he would only burst a vein" ("Two Mc-
Neils," *CP*, 5). "Rumors are thick about him through the circuit.
/ Some say he hates the women, and loves men: / That once,
out West, he tried to kiss a man, / Was badly hurt, then almost
killed himself" ("Gabriel de Ford," *CP*, 7).

> Pretty? Well, if you call it pretty, to have
> That listless scanty flaxen hair, and eyes
> So sentimentally blue. When she was hired,
> She was half-starved, poor thing, and cried and cried,—
> ("Amorosa and Company" *CP*, 9)

The repetition does get wearisome. The irony of outward skill and grace and of the world-weary, petty, hateful emotional innuendo wears thin. Aiken, aware of this effect, occasionally inserts an entirely different note, as in poem XIII of the series (*CP*, 14-16).

> It was that afternoon, early in June,
> When, tired with a sleepless night, and my act performed,
> Feeling as stale as streets,
> We met under dropping boughs, and you smiled to me:
> And we sat by a watery surface of clouds and sky.
>
> (*CP*, 15)

But for the most part, the poems reiterate the hatefulness of the persons performing before his eyes.

> I had to kill him,—that's all,—I had to kill him.
> I told him straight, if he touched me just once more,—
> That way, you know,—I'd kill him. And I did.
>
> . . . .
>
> And seeing that he was done for, I stabbed myself:
> A Jap I knew once showed me how to do it.
> And I heard great bells go roaring down the darkness;
> And a wind rushed after them. And that was all.
> ("Boardman and Coffin," *CP*, 17)

The least that may be said for these poems is that they released Aiken (temporarily) from the sentimentality and the quiet bright rhythms of his earlier verse. The language of *Turns and Movies* is hard, simple, limited usually to the capacities of the persons to whom the poems are addressed. The irony, while there is little to be said for it, has something of the harshness of the graveyard confessionals in *Spoon River Anthology*. Perhaps one can say that Aiken has swung too far away. At any rate, the vaudevillians have almost as limited a range as the "youths" of *Earth Triumphant*. Nothing of the outward grace is communicated, nor are the questions of pride of place, skill, reaction to and relationship with audience, taken up. There is more to be said about these people than is said by them; and to this matter of the "voicing of the inarticulate" Aiken does not attend.

Turns and Movies continues in a series of poems with the general title "Discordants." These seem like minor Yeats or major Housman. The first of them has a loveliness of soft regret that has endeared it to those who know poets from anthologies. The agony of loss through death is expressed so much more skillfully than it was in *Earth Triumphant* as to make the poem momentarily a wonder.

> Music I heard with you was more than music,
> And bread I broke with you was more than bread;
> Now that I am without you, all is desolate;
> All that was once so beautiful is dead.

It is not so much the sentiment, but the intimacy that attracts: "Your hands once touched this table and this silver, / And I have seen your fingers hold this glass . . ." (*CP*, 18).

The other three poems of the series are less effective—a series of rather naked despairs: "My heart has become as hard as a city street" (*CP*, 19); and "Dead Cleopatra was once revered in Egypt, / . . . Now she is very old and dry and faded, . . ." (*CP*, 19). And a despair of separation: "Tumult and madness, desolate for the sea-gulls, / You on the farther shore, and I in this street . . ." (*CP*, 20).

The final poem of *Turns and Movies* ("All Lovely Things," *CP*, 20-21), is a summary Housman statement of the evanescence and impermanence of beauty and joy. Time has a relentless effect on "all lovely things," which must "have an ending," no matter how we try to forestall it:

> Come back, true love! Sweet youth, remain!—
> But goldenrod and daisies wither,
> And over them blows autumn rain,
> They pass, they pass, and know not whither.
>   (20-21)

So far we have seen a verse that has no ideational strength, a verse carried by its technical skill or its sentiment—or failing in both. The fact is that Aiken is still emerging from the nineteenth century and has scarcely gone either into the twentieth or back to the sixteenth and seventeenth centuries. In *Nocturne of Remembered Spring*,[15] he did try to make the turn, but the poems are not distinguished. In his Preface to *Collected Poems*, Aiken explains why he has kept only one of these poems: "it was difficult to find anything worth keeping: the one specimen here exhibited ["Episode in Grey," pp. 21-25] will serve as a sufficient example of the lengths to which an obsession with the 'musical' analogies of poetry could be carried. . . ."

Not only the "musical analogies," but the echoes of Aiken's contemporaries disturb the reader. Much of the volume echoes the sentiments of *Earth Triumphant*—as in the title "Nocturne" (11-17): moonlight on the landscape, memory playing upon experience, the dread of aging and death, etc. There are "musical analogies" here, as in "Episode in Grey": a repetition of lines, echoes of musical instruments, varying of rhythms, all designed to "duplicate" music in verse. The same devices are apparent in "Meditation on a June Evening" (*Nocturne*, 18-26): "Music persuades and captures the subtlest air. . . / As evening comes, my thoughts turn back to you" (19). Perhaps the following lines are Aiken at his very worst:

> The wry-faced moon goes leering up the sky.
> The roofs are shiny, the fountain shoots and falls
> Against the stars, ringed with a ring of foam
> The stars are tittering in the skies.
>
> (25)

The mood varies in "1915: The Trenches" (*Nocturne*, 30-38), in which he responds to war; but the poem is interesting only as a measure of Aiken's failure to accommodate the thought of evil. The sentiment is a common enough literary reaction to World War I: "This vast symphonic dance of death, / This incoherent dust" (32) shuts off beauty, gives us "No tenderness to stay our hands" (35). There is much anger over evil and destruction, and in the manner of John Dos Passos' early heroes. But Aiken is still inclined to separate beauty and evil too easily, and the attitudes he takes toward each do not appreciate the complexity of their relationships. It is a feeling not unlike that of a superficial Emersonian man, who may be shocked but can-

not abide the thought of evil. Aiken's poem is not likely to
threaten the position of Ezra Pound's *Hugh Selwyn Mauberley*
(1920), poems 4 and 5, as the supreme poetic statement of anger
over World War I.

The imitation of Eliot begins in "Sonata in Pathos" (*Nocturne*,
39-46), an almost literal repetition of the language in "The Love
Song of J. Alfred Prufrock"

> Well, I am tired . . . tired of all these years,
> The hazy mornings, the noons, the misty evenings,
> Tired of the spring, tired of the fall;
> The music starts again, I have heard it all,
>
> (39)

It proceeds in an echo of "La Figlia Che Piange": a thought of
what he might miss, were she dead

> You would have been my friend, my more than friend
>
> .   .   .   .
>
> (43)
>
> Perhaps it is death alone whom I shall love.
> (44)

But the Eliotic touch dissolves into something else when associated with Aiken's too frequently equating moonlight and music.
The association is prolonged *ad nauseam* in "White Nocturne"
(*Nocturne*, 47-56): the "magic of white / Touching and changing all familiar things" (48). This may suggest John Gould
Fletcher's "Symphonies," but Fletcher calculates and varies his
effects much more successfully.

Once again, in "Nocturne in a Minor Key" (*Nocturne*, 59-64),
the language of Prufrock is imitated. The hesitations of Prufrock,
his unwillingness to commit himself for fear that the woman will
not care, or will scorn him are here repeated. His thoughts
"whirl like windy papers under streetlamps" (59; cf. Eliot's
Preludes, I). Finally, the narrator "directs" the woman to pose
for him in an attitude suitable to his mood.

> Be patient, press your palm against my heartbeats,
> Reverse my heart like an hour-glass,
> And watch the downward sifting of my minutes
> Until the time when I must pass . . .

You shall have heard, at least, a poignant music
And seen futility;
You will know better than to weep for me.

(60)

V

So much of this early verse is inconsequential that it may be necessary to defend spending so much time discussing it. Surely the sources of both Aiken's weakness and his strength are evident here. The very qualities of his early verse that make it unacceptable are those that—in altogether different forms and uses—gave strength to his later poetry. The "emptiness" of these "Nocturnes" comes less from a lack of talent than from a failure to make good use of his gifts. There is a sign of weariness with apprenticeship in *Nocturne of Remembered Spring:* a feeling that something different and something more need to be done with these effects.

We should remember also that in the years of the volumes discussed in this chapter, Aiken is busy at reading and reviewing his contemporaries. He checks them against his verse, is attracted to what resembles it, then notes weaknesses in it, the sense of a dead-end of technique; and he admires (and imitates, as we have seen) a poetry very different from his, Eliot's.

The most important aspect of his growth in these years is not so much in the search for new directions in poetry, as in giving himself ideational support. The early poetry has *no* intellectual substance; and the emotions therefore become tenuously romantic moods, like the worst of Verlaine, or a *fin de siècle* condition of suspension. It is not that a "body of thought" needs to be inserted in, or used to prop, the verse; it is that a sense of both psychological and metaphysical precision needs to be present, or the verse is in danger of fading away.

There is some evidence in these early poems that at least the necessity of these qualities is appreciated. Aiken experiments first with ideas and fancies that are not his. Then he elaborately plays upon moods that cannot be sustained at length. Dissatisfied with these, he tries a form of "romantic naturalism," with conscious ironies affected by Masters, which soon wear thin. The echoes of early Eliot are not so important (their strength is after all dissolved in moonlight) as the fact of Eliot's presence.

It is strange to see—from the evidence of *Ushant* and from Aiken's reviews—that he sees something in Eliot that Eliot does not himself care to see. The emotional values put, for example, upon *The Waste Land* in Aiken's review of it are very different from those Eliot wants to see in it himself. It is the analysis of self in F. H. Bradley's *Appearance and Reality*—to which Eliot turned his attention in his doctoral dissertation—that attracts Aiken: not Bradley's implications, but his statements concerning the isolation of selves from one another. Such commentary as the one Eliot included to illustrate one of the closing lines of *The Waste Land* is relevant:

> My external sensations are no less private to myself than are my thoughts or my feelings. In either case my experience falls within my own circle, a circle closed on the outside; and, with all its elements alike, every sphere is opaque to the others which surround it. . . . In brief, regarded as an existence which appears in a soul, the whole world for each is peculiar and private to that soul.[16]

The peculiar isolation of selves from one another—not dissipated by any of Bradley's Kantian impulses—is a fact both of empirical philosophy and psychology and of turn-of-the-century romanticism. In the latter case, it was helped along both by a recourse to Nietzschean dramatics (isolation in the popular sense becomes a sign of superiority, as in Aiken's novel, *King Coffin*) and by inferences from Freudian psychology. From the 1890's and the succeeding decade, Aiken borrowed the more insubstantial poses of romantic isolation; these sufficed him, as did a wearisome "I-love-life" bravado, for a time. But, ultimately, he was to get back to the elementary facts of self, as empirically examined in Hume and elsewhere, and for a time he dramatized in the concise imagery of Eliot's *Prufrock and Other Observations* and "Gerontion." Aiken stopped short of the temptation—clearly seen in "Gerontion" and *The Waste Land*—to invest the dilemma of the self with suggestions of religious meaning. The "I" of Aiken's poetry is quite free of either the obligations or the privileges of religious association. His position is therefore much more hazardous, but it is also "privileged" in its isolation.

I do not intend to suggest that this position is more than remotely given in the early poems. Perhaps their genuine con-

tribution is to demonstrate—both to Aiken and to his readers—
its *necessity*. When we speculate upon the variety of ways in
which the sense of void, of the abyss, is communicated in
modern poetry, the strategies used by Aiken become all the
more interesting. Baudelaire talked of "original sin"; Rimbaud
of an inverted angelism; Verlaine returned gratefully to the
church; Eliot had recourse to the Anglican past; Pound, to an
idealized institutionalism. None of these attracted Aiken.

He was, of course, fascinated by the mixture of comic irony,
dramatic assertion, and essential sadness, of the Laforguian Pier-
rot and the gestures of comical contempt in the clown's and
puppet's occasional defiance of "the truth." His "Nocturnes,"
devitalized versions of Laforgue's "Pierrots," bear the same relation to his later poetry as the sense of bravado in the *Earth Triumphant* poems bears to the mature ontology of the *Preludes*.

It would be wrong, I think, to say that the early poems were
"false starts"; they were beginnings, but the direction toward
which they prove eventually to point must scarcely then have
been evident. The immaturity of the early verse was not different
from that which usually afflicts a poet—who, if he has enough
time, can work his way out of it; except, perhaps, the process
lasted longer than it commonly does in the case of Aiken.

The "Symphonies" are transitional. They are contemporary,
or almost contemporary, with the *Nocturnes*, and not much later
than *Earth Triumphant*. In them, Aiken explored a number
of ways—formal, dramatic, "musical"—of righting himself; he
dropped the ineptitudes of his earlier stances, and he put the
musical thematics of the "Nocturnes" to a profitable and significant use.

CHAPTER 4

The Symphonies

I

IN the "Symphonies" Conrad Aiken attempted both a conception of observer-hero and an experiment in form. As for the
first, the common ground of observation is the self contem-
plating the universe through a glass that, while not a mirror,
nevertheless reflects himself within the universe he is observing.
Stanley Kunitz, reviewing the poetry in the *Nation* (October 14,
1931), quotes from David Hume's *Treatise of Human Nature*
to the effect that we are "nothing but a bundle or collection of
different perceptions, which succeed each other with an inconceivable rapidity, and are in a perpetual flux and movement. . . ."[1] This suggests, not that the symphonies are a poetic
version of Hume, but simply that the *Treatise* is one of a series
of speculations which explain the disposition of knower to known.

A more important clue to the self is the figure of the stage,
on which the observer-actor plays out in pantomine and occasionally with monologue what he makes of what he sees. The
situation is not unlike that described in Wallace Stevens' poem,
"Of Modern Poetry" (1940).

> . . . The actor is
> A metaphysician in the dark, twanging
> An instrument, twanging a wiry string that gives
> Sounds passing through sudden rightnesses, wholly
> Containing the mind, below which it cannot descend,
> Beyond which it has no will to rise.[2]

The actor, player, artist, clown (the self has a number of
personae) is continually testing the reality of what he senses, by
converting it into shapes his mind can grasp. To give him authen-

ticity, Aiken changes his form and type from poem to poem. The emotional values similarly moderate. In fact, they change so quickly and are the victims of so many variegations of form that it is difficult to individualize the *personae* of the poems. Aiken was (in 1931 and 1936) to reduce his roles and eliminate the baggage of his "traveling company of performing selves," in the manner advised by Kunitz, who said that he must first "tire of the perpetual vaudeville of his brain and drive from the theatre his company of jugglers, acrobats, and clowns, living himself with the alone."[3]

As for the method of the symphonies, it is described in Aiken's 1919 essay, "Counterpoint and Implication," which he reprinted as an Appendix to the *Collected Poems*.[4] He speaks first of the range of denotation and connotation in poetry: any artist "continually wanders up and down this gamut, striking now at the denotative and now at the connotative chords, never perfectly certain, in fact, which method is the more truly effective; and, of course, obeying not merely a theory but, quite as often, the dictates of compulsions more unconscious" (ABC, 127).

As for the "music" of this poetry, we have already touched upon it;[5] but it will be interesting to see, in the light of the discussion to follow, Aiken's speculations over the patterning of themes:

> . . . (let us for convenience represent any five such simple poetic tones, each composing one separate movement to be used in a symphony, as a, b, c, d, e); but, since one is using them as parts of a larger design, one can also obtain novel effects by placing them in juxtaposition as consecutive movements: such as ab, ac, cae. For a, it is clear, if it is preceded by c and followed by e, is not quite the same as a standing alone. . . .
> . . . One should regard this or that emotional theme as a musical unit having such-and-such a tone quality, and use it only when that particular tone quality is wanted . . . (ABC, 128-29).

This, of course, appears to set a difficult, if not an impossible task. The question has been raised again and again by Poe, by Sidney Lanier, and by the *symbolistes* who tried to describe a poetry corresponding to Richard Wagner's music. It is partly a matter of the poet's wanting to expand form and at the same time to retain a central lyricism; this objective leads to the play and counter-play of certain images and to a constant shifting and flowing of both their original natures and their poetic setting.

T. S. Eliot, in a 1942 essay on "The Music of Poetry," speaks of the sense of rhythm and the sense of structure as "the properties in which music concerns the poet most nearly. . ." He wrote: ". . . There are possibilities for verse which bear some analogy to the development of a theme by different groups of instruments; there are possibilities of transitions in a poem comparable to the different movements of a symphony or a quartet; there are possibilities of contrapuntal arrangement of subject-matter."[6]

There is a constant struggle between melody and meaning. Eliot's remarks at no time suggest the sacrifice of meaning. John Crowe Ransom has elaborately charted the tension of "determinate" and "interdeterminate" meanings and sounds in a line or stanza or the totality of a poem.[7] One may imagine the extreme of "indeterminateness" as represented by the "colour effects" in some of the poems of John Gould Fletcher:

Whirlpools of purple and gold,
Winds from the mountains of cinnabar,
Lacquered mandarin moments, palanquins swaying and balancing
Amid the vermilion pavilions, against the jade balustrates;
Glint of the glittering winds of dragon-flies in the light;
Silver filaments, golden flakes settling downwards;
Rippling, quivering flutters; repulse and surrender,
The sun broidered upon the rain,
The rain rustling with the sun.

("Irradiations," I, stanza I)

The successive gradations of image, and the repetition of phrases in the work of Amy Lowell, are an additional evidence:

I walk down the garden paths,
And all the daffodils
Are blowing, and the bright blue squills.
I walk down the patterned garden paths
In my stiff brocaded gown.
With my powdered hair and jewelled fan,
I too am a rare
Pattern, as I wander down
The garden paths.

("Patterns," lines 1-9)

Of course these are mere demonstration *tours de force;* they
have humble objectives and depend upon relatively simple
ideational matters. What happens to these images when the
poet has major ambitions for them? Is the melody to be sacri-
ficed to the meaning, or the meaning to the melody, or can
both be held in balance? What happens to the dramatic or to
the intellectual matter in exercises of this kind if they are continued and expanded? Aiken points to this danger, in the essay
cited above:

> . . . the danger, I mean, that one's use of implication will
> go too far, and that one will cheat the natural human appetite
> for something solid and palpable. One cannot, truly, dine—at
> least every evening—on, as Eliot would remark, "smells of
> steaks in passageways." One must provide for one's symphony
> a sufficiently powerful and pervasive underlying idea—and,
> above all, make it sufficiently apparent . . . (ABC, 130).

II

Whether he was able to avoid the danger in the "Symphonies,"
we shall have to see. In the pattern offered in his rearrangement
of them in 1949 in *The Divine Pilgrim,*[8] they follow this order:
The Charnel Rose (1918), *The Jig of Forslin* (1916), *The House
of Dust* (1920), *Senlin* (1918), *The Pilgrimage of Festus* (1923),
and *Changing Mind* (written in 1925). The order is that of
composition, not of publication; they were written, except for the
"Coda," between 1915 and 1920.

In *The Divine Pilgrim* some of them are considerably revised,
some shortened. The arrangement is obviously in terms of a
"general project," what Aiken called (speaking of the first, second, and fourth titles) "The problem of personal identity, the
struggle of the individual for an awareness of what it is that con-
stitutes his consciousness; an attempt to place himself, to relate
himself to the world of which he feels himself to be at once an
observer and an integral part" (ABC, 130). The theme (which
is here specifically applied to *Senlin*) is applicable in varying
stresses and strengths to the series as a whole.

The Charnel Rose[9] underwent "severe treatment" in preparation for *The Divine Pilgrim:* ". . . An almost indispensable part
of the general scheme of the poem, and therefore to be salvaged

if at all possible, its youthful exuberance and rhetoric, its Blue Flower romanticism and Krafft-Ebing decadence (although admittedly for a purpose) presented after thirty-three years [1915-1948] an almost insoluble problem in surgery" (*CP*, 863).

The shifting, varying masks assumed by "man in general" as he seeks, tastes, and rejects experience, prompted such critics as Stanley Kunitz to speak of the hero of the "Symphonies" as "a pathetic, rusty-haired little fellow who eternally sits at a window, chin propped up in his hands, sleeves fuzzy at the elbows—eternally sits and dreams through the pane. . . . all that remains for the observer is a confused awareness of the major tragedy of minor souls."[10] The effect is of the "Nocturnes," a moving in and out of moonlight, seeing and hearing "nothing at all." The protagonist, "who sought forever unsatisfied," ". . . caught at the rays of the moon, yet found but darkness,"

> Caught at the flash of her feet, to fill his hands
> With the sleepy pour of sands.
>
> (*CP*, 27-28)

The conventional symbol of this search for beauty is the rose, which almost before the eyes declines and dies:

> He watched red roses drop apart
> Each to disclose a charnel heart.
>
> (*CP*, 29)

This motif is repeated again and again, a major theme of the "symphony." Roses, he thought, "were kin to her, / Pure text of dust. . . ." And, though he heard music within the area of his quest, it too was fleeting, "A fugitive and amazing thing" (*CP*, 31). He is looking for, at, within himself. The *persona* of these poems is frequently staring at himself in a mirror, in a pane of glass, in the wide world itself.

> His own face leered at him, with timid lust,
> Was overwhelmed in night.
> He turned aside, and walked in graveyard dust,—
>
> (*CP*, 32)

In this case, he is looking at his own death, or at the inevitable death of all living, growing things; he fights against the prospect, but cannot avoid the process of aging, of turning to dust. The corruption of the body seems also to drag with it the "soul"—the forms of beauty, of apparent grandeur and permanence.

> But roses fell through the darkness,
> They writhed before him out of the mould,
> Opened their hearts to pour out darkness,
> Darkness of flesh, of lust grown old.
> He struggled against them, beat,
> Broke them with hands to feel the blood flow warm,
> Reeled, when they opened their hearts,
> Feeling them with their eyes closed push and swarm,
> Thronging about his throat, pressing his mouth,
> Beating his temples, choking his breath. . . .
>
> (*CP*, 33)

This is the essential heart of the poem: the struggle with death, the refusal to give in to it. In Part II his search involves exploring the prospects of love as an insurance against death. The illusion is that youth would remain forever "ringed with flame";

> But at times it seemed,
> Walking with her of whom he subtly dreamed,
> (Music beneath the sea)
> That she was texture of earth no less than he;
>
> (*CP*, 35)

He persists nevertheless in his illusion, thrusting aside religion and the solaces of the gods. The imperative pressing upon the Aiken hero is to remain within a secular discourse; disillusionment is, therefore, inevitable.

> These are my hands, that tremble upon your face,—
> Trembling lest love depart from our shadowy place;
> Lest suddenly in my arms you become a sea
> Laughing, with numberless waves, to murder me.
>
> (38)

The evidence of death is overwhelming. The world is a "charnel rose." Watching the night fall, he is reminded of the quiet cessation of life, of its being horribly menaced by death at every turn.

He turned, and saw the world go down behind him,
Into the sounding darkness;
Voices out of tumult cried to remind him,
Wailed, and were lost in wind;

(*CP*, 40)

He is determined to seek out life in its full, garish, deep colors:
red, the color of blood, "the color of steap sun seen through eye-
lids."

Madness for red! I devour the leaves of autumn.
I tire of the green of the world.
I am myself a mouth for blood.

(41)

But the color of blood and the color of lust are again confusedly
mixed with the color of death.

Yet, it is strange—behind that altar,
Carved with cold foam of time,
Skeletons lay: I saw them in the dusk.
Shells winked between the ribs, and over the hands
Rippled the obedient sands.

(*CP*, 46)

The Charnel Rose is a continuous play upon this theme:
love–death, beauty–decay, the delusion of power over human
finalities. The protagonist is identified only as "he" and "I"; the
quest and the disenchantment are both universal; and they are
mirrored in the inevitable changes in all matter, the rising and
dying of the sun, and the disintegration of the rose into dust,
suggestions of Eliot's "ash on an old man's sleeve."

As in several other places in Aiken's writings, the protagonist
turns to the Christ image, which seems alone to have offered
a promise of conquest over death. The protagonist indulges in a
fantasy of resurrection: "Let us delude ourselves that dust may
rise, / That earth relents at last" (*CP*, 49).

He turned in the dusk, and saw none coming behind him;
He listened, and heard no sound.
"I am Christ!" he cried. His words were lost in the silence.

. . . .

"I am Christ!" he cried. A whisper of leaves denied him.

(*CP*, 50)

The illusion of the third day deceives no one. Despite his desperate reminder that this thing had happened before, somewhere, he cannot convince himself, or others, of it.

> Laughter rushed round him; they spat upon his face;
> They struck him and beat him down.
> Thinking him dead, they left him in that place:
> Lying against an old wall, crushed and bleeding,
> With lamplight on his face.

(*CP*, 51)

And the poem ends on the note with which it began. The day sets, the darkness crowds in upon the living, the rose turns to dust, the blood of love is the blood-color of the setting sun.

The Jig of Forslin[11] is a much more ambitious and varied work. Here for the first time in the series Aiken has recourse to the stage figure, or clown figure, who does more than "seek"; he actively mimics life and invites disaster. Aiken called the poem "an exploration of [the hero's] emotional and mental hinterland, his fairyland of impossible illusions and dreams: ranging, on the one extreme, from the desire for a complete tyranny of body over mind, to the desire, on the other extreme, for a complete tyranny of mind over body . . ." (*CP*, 866).

Forslin, emerging from his dream, remembers only one fragment of it:

> An old man lurching slowly out of darkness,
> A bag upon his shoulders growing monstrous . . .
> Now he is gone, before I see his face.
> I am spread upon a fog, and know no plan.

(*CP*, 57-58)

The old man is, of course, himself; he has recourse to memory, where as a youth he did nothing but juggling; now "growing older, I wanted something better. / To do the impossible! . . ." (58).

There is more than a suggestion of Wallace Stevens' Crispin here and in other "Symphonies."[12] Forslin, like Crispin, greets

the changes in the phenomenal world with appropriate gestures
—or with what seem to be such. Forslin had, for example, spent
all his time in practicing his balancing trick, as if that were an
ultimate figure. And it almost becomes so: from balancing "the
one ball on the other" he turns to the ambition to balance worlds.
The perfection of "his act," so that it may be the best of its
kind, becomes an absorbing occupation—until he suddenly loses
confidence in it and in the meaning he has so urgently forced
upon it.

> There's the curtain falling—and I am over.
> I will breathe gas tonight in a locked room,
> And forget those faces . . . .
>
> (*CP*, 60)

In addition, there is a desire to translate things into music
in the manner of Stevens' Peter Quince: "Things mused upon are,
in the mind, like music" (64). But mostly it is Forslin in the
acts of juggling and balancing, setting forces (as he imagines and
reduces them) against one another, trying to "stay" the world
against his life. He has tried everything: "Once I loved; and
once I died; and once / I murdered my lover. . ."

> Once I stepped from the threshold, and saw my body
> Huddled in purple snow.
> Once I escaped my flesh and rose on starlight.
> The theme returns. We bow our hearts and go.
>
> (*CP*, 67)

A succession of murders flash through his mind: once I murdered "a priest, before his altar, / With his own crucifix—";
again, I murdered, "by the waterfront: / A drunken sailor, in a
peg-house brawl . . ." (74). He sees a procession of coffins pass
by, death in the city streets, in houses of pleasure, in the open
fields: the crime of passion, the crime for profit, the gratuitous
crime. All of these images are an effort to participate actively
in events that occur anyway, whether he initiates them or not.
    Part III introduces (or intrudes?) the world of mermaids and
lamias. They, half one thing and half another, are both "monstrous miscarriages" of life who have a lulling or a poisonous

influence; in any case, they remove the hero from normal participation in life.

> She narrowed her eyelids, and fixed her eyes,
> Fiercely upon me; and searched me so
> With speeding fire in every shred
> That I, consumed with a witching glow,
> Knew scarcely if I were alive or dead:
> But lay upon her breast, and kissed
> The deep red mouth, and drank the breath,
> And heard it gasping, how it hissed
> To mimic the ecstasy of death.
>
> *(CP, 83)*

The introduction of these weird creatures is to emphasize the monstrous character of all life, however normal it may seem. Death superintends all existence, "And a skeleton leers upon us in evening dress . . ." (87).

Again, Aiken roams freely through all available myths and legends, though each is reduced to examination by skeptical eyes. Was Christ "a god, perhaps, or devil?" (*CP*, 90). And the story of the passion is given; Forslin walks painfully—with and as Christ—up the hill to crucifixion: "Jesus is whipped for being slow, / The great cross pains his shoulders so" (97). Forslin is both crucifier and crucified. Like the two persons in Aiken's short story "The Disciple,"[13] he is both Christ and Judas.

> "He writhes his head from side to side.
> O holy Christ I have crucified!—
> I twist there on the cross with you;
> And what you suffer I suffer too."
>
> (98)

In the final section (Part V) of *Forslin*, the past filters through consciousness. Forslin, no longer so anxiously active, reflects upon the rhythms that "take the blood with magic" and the rhythms "there are that die in the brain's dark chambers" (*CP*, 102). The most sordid images (and the most beautiful, perhaps, in view of Aiken's concern with them) are those of the city streets. Here, in an echo of Eliot's "Rhapsody on a Windy Night," which Aiken so much admired, are the scenic fragments which Forslin stores in his mind:

Music from concertinas in an alley,
And cats with slow green eyes.
                    (*CP*, 110)

.   .   .   .

My veins are streets. Millions of men rush through them
                                                    (111)

.   .   .   .

The walls of the city are rolled away

.   .   .   .

Men in their shirtsleeves reading papers
Women by mirrors combing out their hair.
                    (112)

Forslin sits and meditates upon the variety of changing shapes
he has assumed. They are the shapes of life and history, and
he is simply an observer of "the hurrying days [that] go down
to join the years" (114). Just how much advantage has accrued
from Aiken's having Forslin live a thousand lives, commit a
thousand murders, and die a thousand deaths is a matter of some
doubt. His sensitivity to experience is turned into a ragtag and
bobtail imitation of it.

We are left with the inventory of experience, given this imitative dramatization of it. The strategy is, of course, to make it
a part of the "stage" which is art—so that the particulars succeed
each other in the manner of a pantomimist/impersonator. Presumably both the phenomena and their meaning acquire an
additional value in this way; but the manner is not entirely successful because Forslin has no power of initiative and can only
dance (or act out) what happens and will happen with or without him.

IV

The House of Dust, the third of the series in time of composition,[14] was also much revised, "although not much cut," for
publication in *The Divine Pilgrim*. A preface which does not
appear in the first edition is added, from memory, in the 1949
collection. In it, Aiken speaks of the work as "a symphonic poem
about the city—ancient or modern, it makes no difference—and
the crowd-man that inhabits it."

It is entered by us at twilight, say, we mingle with its casual or ordered currents, and by degrees come to feel something of its anonymous and multicellular identity, an identity which seems to be in effect the fusion or coalescing of the innumerable particles that compose it. These particles, too, at first seem to us to be anonymous and amorphous,—particles and nothing more. But gradually, as we explore and participate further, or empathize more willingly, we begin to see that the particles too have identity, or individuality, that in fact they are more and more perceptible as individuals (*CP*, 868-69).

The object is to identify the city with the consciousness of it—with the "soul" or the "you" or the "I" of Eliot's "Preludes"—though Aiken's poem is made more philosophically ambitious and pretentious, and he has no intention of concluding only with "the notion of some infinitely gentle / Infinitely suffering thing."[15] *The House of Dust* is much too diffuse, extended and repetitive to submit to so simple a "notion" as that.

The entire poem, he says, "is really an elaborate progressive analogy between the city, seen as a multicellular living organism, and the multicellular or multilinear nature of human consciousness." Herein lie the arguments, or excuses, for a secular vision of man. Man becomes divine through the widening of his consciousness; the "macrocosm" and the "microcosm unite; and man can, if he only will, become divine" (*CP*, 869).

It is difficult to see just how much of this argument is actually relevant to the poem. What happens is not that the consciousness of the ego becomes a master of what he expansively sees, but that the observer and the observed alternate until they are fused, or confused, as one object. The intention is clearly enough indicated in the shifting, successive, moderating images of the "multicellular" city in Part I. It is, perhaps as Henry Wells describes it, the "inversion" of Whitman's view of the city,[16] though Whitman had ostensibly the same purpose in offering his catalogues of urban sights and sounds. Aiken's ego dissolves and is reshaped; he absorbs, while Whitman's "I" adds.

> I am dissolved and woven again . . .
> Thousands of faces rise and vanish before me.
> Thousands of voices weave in the rain.
>
> (*Dust*, 23)

The composite urban self participates in a strangely vicarious way in the life of the city: parts of it separate and merge again:

> We descend our separate stairs toward the day,
> Merge in the somnolent mass that fills the street,
> Lift our eyes to the soft blue space of sky,
> And walk by the well-known walls with accustomed feet.
>
> *(Dust,* 33)

There is no effort to transcend these facts—no visionary leap toward mystic meaning such as we note in Hart Crane's "For the Marriage of Faustus and Helen."[17] All adventures are dissipated in this common absorption, which is passive; it is active only in the effort to comprehend, compare, and assimilate.

> My peril goes out from me, is blown among you.
> We loiter, dreaming together, along the street.
>
> *(Dust,* 40)

The poem dips in and out of specific lives, fragments of speech and acts, and then it moves back again to the generalities that serve them:

> Two lovers, here at the corner, by the steeple,
> Two lovers blow together like music blowing:
> And the crowd dissolves about them like a sea.
> Recurring waves of sound break vaguely about them,
> They drift from wall to wall, from tree to tree.
>
> *(Dust,* 45)

The very flatness of the language is deliberate, forbidding as it does any temptation to make metaphysical "capital" of it. We may have a better sense of this deliberate simplicity, if we compare, for example, these lines from Part I of Hart Crane's poem:

> There is some way, I think, to touch
> Those hands of yours that count the nights
> Stippled with pink and green advertisements.
> And now, before its arteries turn dark,
> I would have you meet this bartered blood.
> Imminent in his dream, none better knows
> The white wafer cheek of love, or offers words
> Lightly as moonlight on the eaves meets snow.
>
> *(Collected Poems,* 94)

Crane's hero joins Helen in a union of persons and gods, which lifts them both above "the stacked partitions of the day" (*Collected Poems*, 93). The "I" of Aiken's *The House of Dust*, however, is held within the limits of the earth and death. "Death, from street to alley, from door to window, / Cries out his news —of unplumbed worlds approaching" (*Dust*, 84). But there is some effort to rise from the dust, and it is consonant with Aiken's stated aim in the Preface. The argument assumes the form of Robinson's "Man Against the Sky": Is dust the only answer? If it is, "what were the use, you ask?" (*Dust*, 92).

The fact remains that the composite "I" has an especially burdensome task: to remain faithfully and honestly what he is, to lift his mind above the dust. But the ethical imperative is a "ghost," an echo of the unconscious wish for "design."

> I am content to say, "this world is ordered,
> Happily so for us, by accident:
> We go our ways untroubled save by laws
> Of natural things." Who makes the more assumption?
> (*Dust*, 94)

The typical gesture of the hero is to rise (act, gesture, walk forth, stretch out his arms) momentarily and hesitantly, then to sink once more into the cellular mass. ". . . We suddenly rise in darkness, / Open our eyes, cry out, and sleep once more" (*Dust*, 113). The poem closes in a cinematographic survey of the city: sights, sounds, music, the changes from dark to light to dark again. The effect of this movement is to leave the ego distraught and full of hate:

> Now all the hatreds of my life have met
> To hold high carnival . . . we do not speak,
> My fingers find the well-loved throat they seek,
> And press, and fling you down . . . and then forget.
> (*Dust*, 143)

There is no cause for mystic worship, no break in the "partitions of the day," but only a ghostly sense of the city's structure and of its inevitable decline and deterioration into dust.

Houston Peterson reacts to *The House of Dust* as "an adventurous and beautiful achievement," and he admires its having come before the conceptions of *The Waste Land*, as well as "such prose renderings of a city's essence as *Ulysses, City Block, Mrs. Dalloway,* and *Manhattan Transfer*" (*Melody,* 97). Whether precedence is a virtue or not, the fact is that *The House of Dust* is inferior to all of the works mentioned with the possible exception of Waldo Frank's *City Block.*

The failure of *The House of Dust* is not so much a matter of point of view as of sharpness in the use of perceptions. Nowhere in Aiken's first "major phase" has his poetry failed him quite so much. There is an uncertainty, a timidity, about the scene's challenge; and the absence of a specific dramatic or symbolic means of giving perspective to the details is seriously damaging. The poem surely fails to fulfill the promise made in the Preface, for there is too much left undone. And, on the other hand, there is much that lies flat on the page, to which nothing is done.

Nor are the ideas of the "symphony" especially helpful. There is an alternating motion of particular and generality, but it is altogether predictable and, therefore, not especially interesting. The problem of creating a literature from city streets is admittedly a difficult one; yet it has been solved, again and again, but only by drawing sharply toward the "specimen selves" and exploiting their individualities, which cannot be seen unless they are approached. There is something to be said for the notion that Aiken's refusal to commit himself to a specific *persona*—his reluctance to make a generalized "consciousness" into a specific sentient being—has inhibited him.

V

Senlin: A Biography[18] may perhaps be thought to answer the complaint about *The House of Dust.* It is not a "symphony" in the sense of its sacrificing precision for thematic effect. It has a *persona* with a name; and the subtitle suggests a form of explicable progression. But the name is as generalized as is Eliot's "Gerontion." There is a comic sense of both eccentricity and commonalty in *Senlin,* which gives it a lightness that *The House of Dust* sadly lacks. Senlin comes closer than any other of Aiken's *personae* to having the qualities of Stevens' *Comedian as the Letter C.* Senlin is, in a sense, on a very similar quest; at least he is bothered by some of Crispin's dilemmas.

Senlin is not an artist, nor the shadow of a prototype of one. He is an ordinary human who tilts with the planet and steadies himself to keep in balance with it. The name, Aiken says in the brief preface to *The Divine Pilgrim* edition of the "Symphonies," "means literally the 'little old man' that each of us must become; just as Forslin, a portmanteau of the Latin words *forsan* and *fors,* is a squinting word which means either chanceling or weakling. . . ." As for the meaning of Senlin, Aiken once again points to the "perennially fascinating problem of personal identity which perplexes each of us all his life: the basic and possibly unanswerable question, *who and what am I,* how is it that I am I, Senlin, and not someone else . . ." (*CP,* 870).

As G. Rostrevor Hamilton has said, *Senlin* "takes us into deep places without being profound,"[19] and this statement suggests a particularly useful way of looking at the poem. The opening is light, quizzical; it undercuts pretension and is a delightful miniature portrait of a figure generalized but real.

> Senlin sits before us, and we see him.
> He smokes his pipe before us, and we hear him.
> Is he small, with reddish hair,
> Does he light his pipe with a meditative stare,
> And a pointed flame reflected in both eyes?
>
> (*CP,* 195)

The philosophical speculation about Senlin, a commonplace in the "Symphonies," consists of the type of query to which we have become accustomed. The mind observing him also observes the universe surrounding him, which is itself, is Senlin, is ourselves:

> Has Senlin become a forest? Do we walk in Senlin?
> Is Senlin the wood we walk in,—ourselves,—the world?
> Senlin! we cry . . . Senlin! again . . . No answer,
> Only soft broken echoes backward whirled . . .
>
> (*CP,* 196)

But Senlin remains himself and walks beside us, swinging his arms and "bending his long legs in a peculiar way, / Goes to his work with thoughts of the universe . . ." (*CP,* 199). He is "happily conscious of his universe," and he finds a profound message in what the tree says in the garden:

> I have sensations, when I stand beneath it,
> As if its leaves looked at me, and could see;
> And these thin leaves, even in windless air
> Seem to be whispering me a choral music,
> Insubstantial but debonair.
>
> *(CP, 200)*

In Part II (called "His Futile Preoccupations"), Senlin speaks in his own person. He describes himself not only as incorporating the particulars of his world (I am a house; I am a city; I am a door, a street, a town), but also somehow as existing quite self-consciously independent of them:

> I arise, I face the sunrise,
> And do the things my fathers learned to do.
> Stars in the purple dusk above the rooftops
> Pale in a saffron mist and seem to die,
> And I myself on a swiftly tilting planet
> Stand before a glass and tie my tie.
>
> *(CP, 206)*

This has an immense power of implication. The balances needed to move the hands and the cloth in a direction different from the planet's are like Forslin's achievement in making one ball balance upon another. Senlin is aware of these accomplishments: he is upright and firm and stands "on a star unstable." He will remember god, and dedicate to him the act of combing his hair.

> Accept these humble offerings, cloud of silence!
> I will think of you as I descend the stair.
>
> *(CP, 206)*

The poem's "symphonic" movements call for a repetition of these phrases. The poem moves toward and away from Senlin, standing aside to observe him, allowing him to observe himself. In either case, the character is comprehended in his relationship to the universe, the universe in its relation to him.

> There are shadows across the windows, clouds in heaven,
> And a god among the stars; and I will go
> Thinking of him as I might think of daybreak
> And humming a tune I know.
>
> *(CP, 207)*

Perhaps god is a giant Senlin? A person who "ties his tie /
Grimacing before a colossal glass of sky?" He speculates upon
god's awakening "from a chaos of starless sleep" (*CP*, 208). He
will think of his work, or of god, identifying the two; perhaps
they are one.

> . . . Nevertheless, I will think of work
> With a trowel in my hands;
> Or the vague god who blows like clouds
> Above these dripping lands . . .
>
> (*CP*, 209)

The theme of death must inevitably enter, since Senlin is an
old man and the thought of it cannot ever be far away. So section 6 of Part II is a pattern of thoughts of death: "I hear the
clack of his feet, / Clearly on stones, softly in dust" (*CP*, 212),
"Cavorting grotesque ecstasies." Senlin does not see him, but
he notes his effects: the lilacs fall, ". . . the scrape of knuckles
against the wall," the spider's "beneficence," and the sense of
haste that the thought of death engenders: that men and women
might live as much as possible before it is too late. He, Senlin,
feels this need to hurry, but he scarcely knows what he should
do, except perhaps to return "To the one small room in the void
I know." At least it was there yesterday: "Will I find it tonight
once more when I climb the stair?" (*CP*, 215).

In the end (Part III, "His Cloudy Destiny"), we are left uncertain. Had Senlin actually existed, or was he only "a dream
we dreamed, and vividly recall"? (*CP*, 222). We know that
"Senlin sat before us and we heard him" (*CP*, 219); but was
his existence any more real to us than the reality of his room
to him? Senlin has dissolved into the natural atmosphere. His
consciousness is no more—unless it has become a part of ours.
The universe persistently resolves itself to Senlin's room:

> Yet, we would say, this is no shore at all,
> But a small bright room with lamplight on the wall;
> And the familiar chair
> Where Senlin sat, with lamplight on his hair.
>
> (*CP*, 220)

The sobering conclusion is that Senlin is all of us, we are
Senlin, the consciousnesses of all merge, and the comprehension

of the universe is a joint progress. But can we not say that we have created Senlin or that Senlin has created his god, whom he imagines in postures and as having sensations similar to his? The poem ends with this reflection.

I should count this poem rather more successful than not, and do so because ideas, conceits, and metaphors rise from the dead sea of repetitive imagery that characterizes *The House of Dust*. *Senlin* gives exactly the kind of specificity that the other poem lacks. We address our attention to him and to his characteristically simple gestures—rising, tying his tie, walking in the sun, smoking, working in the garden; and our questions about his existence are the same questions he poses to himself.

It is not that mythological or special signs are necessarily intrusive but that in so many of Aiken's early poems they tend to translate the meaning from what he has wanted it to be. The association of Forslin with lamias strikes me as gratuitously grotesque. His imagining himself to be Christ is less so, but perhaps only because the application is more appropriate. In any case, Forslin and Senlin play well against each other and help to give the themes of the "Symphonies" some sense of localization, which *The Charnel Rose* is too vague and *The House of Dust* too dully inanimate to offer.

VI

The pattern of these poems, which Aiken has chosen to call *The Divine Pilgrim*, closes pretentiously indeed. *The Pilgrimage of Festus*[20] is an elaborate fantasy on the search for truth and self-knowledge. Once again, Festus is "anybody or nobody" on an imaginary pilgrimage—"a cerebral adventure, of which the motive is a desire for knowledge" (*CP*, 871).

Festus begins "with nothing more to conquer" except knowledge of himself. His confidence at the beginning resembles Crispin's, who had mastered "snails" and "salad beds" but finds the "ubiquitous concussion, slap and sigh"[21] of the sea beyond him. But the confidence of Festus has in it a quality of arrogance; he does not humble himself before the earth but tries to create within it. Having found that mortality tends to nullify pretensions to human power, Festus seeks out the wisdom (in imaginary conversations) with Confucius and the Buddha, with Christ, even with Mephistopheles. He ends only with the suggestion that the prospect of self-exploration pleases.

Mr. Hamilton suggests that *Festus* resembles a pageant, rather too elaborately mounted.[22] It is too lavish for what it wishes to accomplish, but it serves nevertheless as still another way of presenting the themes of the long series of "Symphonies." If it is a pageant, its parts move into line with regularity and precision. Festus in the beginning has decided to explore himself in simple relationship to nature; in short, he chooses to *"cultiver son jardin."*

> Festus, lighting his pipe against the sun,
> Smokes in the furrows, regarding tenderly
> His beans which, one by one,
> Now shoulder through the dark earth sturdily
> (*CP*, 228)

But "the world grows dark," and he is uneasy. The natural truths are insufficient to forestall mortality, which "Down the cold battlements of the west . . . / Dolorously descends" (*CP*, 229). So he attempts to enter the universe itself, to climb "the colossal and savage stairs of the sunlight" (*CP*, 234). His dark dreams sadly reproach him "With unfulfilments . . ." (*CP*, 236). In the deep forest he consults the wisdom of departed spirits. Confucius advises: "Be tranquil, stare at death, / Live as the grass lives, uncomplaining, / Be grateful for the sun." The Buddha asks him to

> "Look through the little whirlings of night and day,
> The dark brief flight of clouds and rain,
> The red transparencies of pleasure and pain,—
> To the white perfection of the infinite . . ."

As for Jesus of Nazareth, He bids him to "love!" (*CP*, 247).

Dissatisfied, he will discourse with Mephistopheles. But all of these meetings are chimeras of his imagination, and Festus is left with "myself alone" (*CP*, 255)—in the "Net of Himself"— struggling somehow to find "some doorway out of the mind!" (*CP*, 262).

> I will not have a god who is myself! . . .
> But the million voices of the grass
> Cry out upon me as I pass . . .

> I will not have a god who is myself!
> But the blue dome of basalt, ice-embossed,
> Carved with hieroglyphs of frost,
> Accuses me.
>
> (*CP*, 260)

The final section is a dialogue between Festus and the Old Man he will become. In the end, he has not been able to escape himself. "The world is the mirror of god; and we are but fragments. / And how shall a mirror look into its own depths, Festus?" (*CP*, 266). But is it not something to have conceived a god?

> How deep this forest of ourselves-in-god!
> How pale the little lanterns of our faces.
>
> (*CP*, 267)

Man, agrees Festus' companion, is a remarkable creature if only because he manages to stay on this planet and in this universe: "That all this whirling lays not hold of us . . ." (*CP*, 268). The wonder of this thought turns Festus away from his discontent; he accepts the challenge of the finite and the infinite clashing and resolving, the stresses and tensions of their paradoxical relationship.

> Then Festus laughed, for he looked in his heart and saw
> His worlds made young again,
> And heard the sound of a many-peopled music,
> And joyously into the world of himself set forward
> Forgetting the long black aftermath of pain.
>
> (*CP*, 275-76)

In reorganizing the "Symphonies," Aiken added the poem "Changing Mind"[23] to represent the "specific 'I'" in a specific predicament: "This predicament, both private and social, of the writer or artist" (*CP*, 872). Presumably, then, "Changing Mind" is the artist looking at Forslin, at Festus, at Senlin, and at himself.

> . . . The wholly anonymous hero of "Changing Mind," . . . and perhaps anonymous with reason, is not only particularized, he is also shown to be the willing participant, and

perhaps to some extent even the instigator, in the process of seeing himself resolved into his constituent particles: and this with a purpose, that his increased awareness may be put at the service of mankind . . . (*CP*, 872-73).

This is an almost perfect statement of Aiken's intention. If the poems themselves do not demonstrate it exactly, it is undoubtedly because the intent is too exactly parochial, too much the superintending monitor of the verse. For "Changing Mind" scarcely serves in the role for which Aiken intended it. It is obvious that the "I" is *different* from the other selves; but the difference is so scrupulously maintained that one had rather (or better) go to them than to seek another dimension or perspective in the "Coda."

Nevertheless, "Changing Mind" is interesting because it points a new direction in Aiken's poetry. The selves are more and more to become "myself"; and eventually they become the poet, or the poet's mind, engaged in the downright, uninterrupted, undramatized exploration of basic problems of "myself alone." It is as though the glass—through which, in the symphonies, he saw the external scene and himself in it looking back at himself—were to become more and more transparent, so that he communicated directly with the scene, and it with him.

Self-consciousness, i.e., narcissism, still dominates "Changing Mind," however.

> "You! Narcissus!" I said!
> And softly, under the four-voiced dialogue,
> In the bright ether, in the golden river
> Of cabbalistic sound, I plunged, I found
> The silver rind of peace, the hollow round
> Carved out of nothing; curled there like a god.
> (*CP*, 277)

The good Doctor Wundt, Aiken's poetic equivalent of the several psychoanalysts of his fiction, assists him in curious ways. For the depths into which the "I" now looks are not only those of the universe but also the caverns and abysses of the psyche. Both external and internal worlds thus require a kind of "*profondeur*," though they are as deep as the poetry will permit them to be. The protagonist (the poet, the artist?) begs "them"

and himself to believe that what he has been able to create is
real:

> . . . O believe, believe!
> Believe, grim four, believe me or I die!
> It is from you this vision comes; while I
> Dreamed that I swam, and with that swimmer came
> Into the southeast of forgotten name.
>
> (*CP*, 283)

"Poem 3," an alternation of prose and poetry, describes a
variety of scenes: a vaudeville theatre, with the seven-man
orchestra tuning up, to entertain "three thousand faces. Faces
in rows like flowers in beds." Here is the relationship of artist
to audience, the work itself designed to assure communication.
And all this, "mind you, was myself!" (*CP*, 283). "I" was everybody: Glozo, the card-eater; Tozo, the Japanese acrobat; Bozo,
the "muscular trapeze artist"; and all the members of the orchestra.

> All this I was, and also the amphitheatre itself,
> All this, but also a small room, a forest,
> Trees full of birds walking down to the water's edge
> Socrates in a basket hanging beside the full moon, eating a partridge,
>
> (*CP*, 284)

The poem concludes with a specialized version of the Lord's
Prayer and the Ave Maria, a purely secular appeal to "My father
which art in earth" and "My mother which art in tomb" (*CP*,
287).

> Father and mother, who gave
> Life, love, and now the grave,
> What is it that I can be?
> Nothing but what lies here,
> The hand still, the brain sere,
> Naught lives in thee
>
> Nor ever will live, save
> It have within this grave
> Roots in the mingled heart,
> In the damp ashes wound
> Where the past, underground,
> Falls, falls apart.
>
> (*CP*, 288)

"What is it that I can be?" This question goes beyond the questionings of the woman in Stevens' "Sunday Morning";[24] and it echoes the sentiment that

> We live in an old chaos of the sun,
> Or old dependency of day and night,
> Or island solitude, unsponsored, free,
> Of that wide water, inescapable.
> (*Complete Poems*, 70)

To examine the full implications of Aiken's "prayer," it is necessary to look back once more upon the ground covered in this chapter. One persistent concept throughout the poetry is that of the mutability of the human species. But Aiken is more than the "gentle hedonist" Julian Symons suggests him to be.[25] He is the ever-questing self, content with nothing but the blankest truth, yet restive on discovering that it is so minimal.

Stevens is grave, somber, and comical by turns in his meditations on mortality; Aiken's verse has the same qualities intermittently, but the sense of the need for definition is more urgent, even at times frantic; and Aiken is much more likely than Stevens to leap audaciously (hysterically) into regions and myths which startle by their obscurity without satisfying their purpose. But both poets begin with the same fundamental necessity: now that my father is in the earth, my mother in her tomb, "What is it that I can be?"

The "Symphonies" display a wide range, an immense versatility, a richness and an almost wasteful brilliance. They lack focus, except occasionally; but they were not conceived, at the beginning at least, as a unity but only as variations on a theme. Reading them in the arrangement Aiken made for *The Divine Pilgrim*, we sense easily enough the relation they have to one another, but we can scarcely say why there should be such an abundance.

Nor can we entirely appreciate the "symphonic" manipulations of "emotion-tones" (the phrase is Aiken's). We have the impression of zig-zag and criss-cross—of a varicolored and impossibly elaborate screen with lines of motion in every which direction. The center is lost—despite the fact that Aiken repeatedly comes back to it—in each of the poems, in his prefatory discussions, and in his "Coda." We feel that the self is the creator of his universe, but also helplessly the victim of it; the swain of death, but also an unrecognizable consequence of its dissolving effects; an artist, a clown, a buffoon, a "little old man," but also a *fin de siècle* Huysmansian connoisseur of decadence.

This may be the "meaningful incoherence" which Aiken once described *The Waste Land* to have and which he defensively attributed to his own work. But it seems to me undeniable that Aiken's imagination is sometimes vagrant without necessarily being far-reaching. This is not to say that the "Symphonies" are not rewarding. They are often a brilliant use of a lavish gift. The substantive intellectual strength is also there, but a bit hard to find; occasionally it is dramatized but in a pretentious or banal way. As is generally true in the history of poets, Aiken was to experiment further with the ideas that were to come from the "Symphonies" to the Preludes; and he did so in lesser, less ambitious, and more discreet poems that are occasionally worth all of the long journey of experiment which led to them.

CHAPTER 5

Maturity

I

BETWEEN the "Symphonies" and the Preludes, Conrad Aiken published a number of poems, two of them elaborate dramatized sketches in the manner of *Forslin* and *Festus*. *Punch: The Immortal Liar*,[1] one of his most popular books, is a dramatic fantasy of the puppet's life and boasts and loves; in it, Aiken utilizes his knowledge of nineteenth-century poetic narrative. Hamilton calls it "a brilliant piece of entertainment," and it is as entertainment that it ought to be judged.

Punch is an "immortal liar" whose vigor of imagination dominates the piece. Several views of his trustworthiness are offered. An old man recalls him as a sneak, a villain, "And yet, somehow, the world seemed greater for him; / Seemed smaller when he died" (*Punch*, 4). Another man of the village, who indignantly denies Punch's nobility, presents an account riddled by superstitious fears and moral righteousness. Punch comes from nowhere:

> . . . A mystery comes among us,
> Ugly and vile beyond all human knowledge,
> A walking vice; he lies, seduces, steals,
> Gets roaring drunk, and leads our youth to mischief.
> The village reeks with him. Corruption rules us.
> (*Punch*, 8)

Punch has his own day "in court." The passage in which his version is given begins in the boomlay spirit of Vachel Lindsay:

> Punch in a beer-house, drinking beer,
> Booms with his voice so that all may hear,
> Bangs on the table with a red-haired fist,
> Writhes in his chair with a hump-backed twist
> (*Punch*, 12)

The achievement either charms or it doesn't. The verse is immensely "accomplished," though the effect may be called wearisomely obvious. Punch tells his story: of his wife and "the others"; of his having caused a furor in town by killing Polly's lover; of his trial, the sentence, his cheating the hangman ("a corpse with a slow green eye / That only lit when he saw men die." *Punch* 19); of his resisting the temptation of the devil; and of his trouble with women:

> Was there in all this wide world never
> One woman I might love for ever?
> Or if that miracle could not be,
> One woman who might tire of me
> Before I tired, and fling me by.
>
> (*Punch,* 29)

The devil's bargain is finally sealed; he agrees to provide such a woman and will collect his soul if Punch doesn't succeed with her. The "immortal liar" succeeds in "interesting" the Queen of Sheba. No man or woman, god or devil, has bested him; Punch concludes: even death, perhaps, though ". . . I'll not say that the time must come / When Death will find me, and leave me dumb!" (*Punch,* 37).

So much for the master liar. Other testimonies refute his. Polly "took him up" to spite his wife Judy; and it was Polly who forced Judy's suicide, from wounded pride. The poem concludes from the perspective of the creator. Punch is seen reduced, humpbacked, long-nosed, ugly; his lying assumes the form of a rhetoric of compensation.

> Red-faced, lascivious, hump-backed, and a coward!
> Where the strings pulled, he moved. He was a puppet.
>
> (*Punch,* 60)

He is presented as pitifully small and inadequate, yet as somehow comically braving it out. The poem closes, and the puppets recede into the mind of their maker. It is a universe within a universe: the puppet-maker, who has a god, is a god of his own, ruling over his creatures.

> He saw himself,—though a god, the puppet of gods;
> Revolving in antics the dream of a greater dreamer;
> Flung up from a sea of chaos one futile instant,

To look on a welter of water whirling with crimson;
And then, in an instant, drawn back once more into chaos.
                                        (*Punch*, 77)

Priapus and the Pool[2] describes the tortures of the flesh, the
ambiguities of our enslavement to its desires.

Are we never to be left by our desires,
But forever try to warm our foolish hearts
At these illusory fires?

                                        (*CP*, 383)

The mythical Priapus can of course be seen two ways: as a god
of fertility, of gardens and herds; as a grotesque and deformed
phallic symbol. The latter is (expectedly) used here. The pre-
vailing tension is that between the permanence of stone and
the wavering identity of the rippling pool. Throughout, there is
the familiar competence, even brilliance—unfavorable criticisms
invariably use the word "facility"—of rhymes, forms, words; but
there is also the same lack or loss of substance.

The development is predictable: how long does beauty last?
how can it be made to seem permanent? why do the shape of
the leaf and the song of the thrush not continue? Time intervenes: the hours "Fall whitely and silently and slowly between
us." (*CP*, 388); the "atomy spectral coffin" darkly passes (*CP*,
391); beauty unaccountably disappears, "gone like a tracery out
of the sky!" (*CP*, 393). The death of beauty forces the poet into
a dreadful state of hateful indecision. He begs either that the
beauty be dissipated, or that he be permitted to hate it.

Or else let hatred like a lightning come,
And flash, and strike it numb,
And strew on rock
These singing leaves, that, singing, seem to mock.
Thus let my heart once more be naked stone,
Bare under wind and hard with grief,
And leave not in a single crevice
A single leaf.

                                        (*CP*, 396)

The language has improved; the rhymes do not appear so
anxiously strained; the curve of thought is smoother. But the
substance is still limited; the subject is still a "posed agony,"

helped on by resources from classical stores. We feel it necessary to say "neatly conceived and well performed," for Aiken is
apparently still convinced that an idea must be "performed" if
it is to be worth anything. The devices, contrivances, and tropes
stand in the way of the vision.

Much the same may be said of *John Deth: A Metaphysical
Legend.*[3] Houston Peterson has described the source of its idea.
Early in 1922, when Aiken was living in the town of Winchelsea,
England, he came upon "the enchanting fact that among the
first three grantees of land under royal charter, about 1289, were
John Deth, Juliana Goatibed, and Millicent Piggistaile." The
opportunities for an extravagant pun were obvious.

Aiken seems to have admitted to a dream he had the night of
the discovery; in it "the dance of death" was localized: "my
Deth would have two complementary figures, one of whom
would symbolize (very roughly) consciousness, while the other
would symbolize the unconscious or the merely physical."
Though he admitted that "My meaning was, and has largely
remained, obscure to me," he did try to specify it:

> "Deth and Piggistaile are the two poles, negative and positive;
> and Goatibed is their joint consciousness, who with especial
> keenness is aware of the necessity for annihilation. Piggistaile
> is a plus sign, Deth is a minus sign: Goatibed is their coefficient.
> They are doomed to an infinite and wearisome repetition of their
> ritual . . ." (*Melody,* 205).

The "Others" of both John Deth and Priapus offer more profitable sources of examination because of our interest in Aiken's
growth to maturity. In the shorter poems a fantasy has less opportunity to turn grotesque, and its precise relevancy is occasionally more sharply revealed. "The Road" (*CP,* 452-54) describes, with fleeting suggestion of Kafkan irony, a village tradition, zealously and painfully followed; the hardships of the
road-building are endured from generation to generation, but
the road itself leads nowhere.

"Dead Leaf in May" (*CP,* 454-55) analyzes the relationship
of ripeness to death in the manner of Frost's "Design," but far less
skillfully:

> Human, who trudge the road from Here to There:
> Lock the dry oak-leaf's flimsy skeleton
> In auricle or ventricle; sail it

> Like a gay ship down red Aorta's flood.
> Be the paired blossoms with dead ribs between.
> Thirst in the There, that you may drink the Here.
>
> (*CP*, 455)

"The Room" (*CP*, 460-61) is one of those rare perfections in which the conceit is developed meaningfully without a waste of syllable or sound.[4] It demonstrates further the slow growth of an independent vision. The symbols that were there since 1914—but seemed so often to be hindered by esoteric baggage—are here begining their journey to a special poetic use, and realization. Even the similar conceit of "Dead Leaf in May" is "used" for sermonizing, as in that poem's last stanza. "The Room" contains no such overt instructions.

Here is Senlin's room without Senlin, with no one but an observer, who only remarks. The room is "ribbed," fashioned, structured, as is the leaf. The two alternate and then fuse.

> Through that window—all else being extinct
> Except itself and me—I saw the struggle
> Of darkness against darkness. . . .

The struggle is between creativity and destruction, both phases of a doom. But the doom itself is "order"; the processes of nature are like those of art.

> . . . Then I saw
> How order might—if chaos wished—become:
> And saw the darkness crush upon itself,
> Contracting powerfully; . . .
>
> (*CP*, 460)

The creative forces within chaos are like those within the human consciousness; the room and the leaf are one. The scene undergoes a remarkable inversion: the leaf invades the room, becomes the room, becomes the tree, of which it is the perfect minuscule sign.

> For the leaf came,
> Alone and shining in the empty room;
> After a while the twig shot downward from it;
> And from the twig a bough; and then the trunk,
> Massive and coarse; and last the one black root.

> The black root cracked the walls. Boughs burst the window:
> The great tree took possession.

The wonder of creation silences the sound of pain. The grief associated with destruction is necessary with the joy of creativity.

> . . . Then turn, have courage,
> Wrap arms and roots together, be convulsed
> With grief, and bring back chaos out of shape.
> I will be watching then as I watch now.
> I will praise darkness now, but then the leaf.
>
> (*CP*, 461)

The idea of this poem is extracted from the sentiment of many others: for example, from these lines of "Sound of Breaking" (*CP*, 461-62): "The sound of disaster and misery, the sound / Of passionate heartbreak at the centre of the world." But the best way to see "The Room" is to contrast it with the superficially lovely "Music I heard with you was more than music" of the first poem of "Discordants" (*CP*, 18).[5] The contrast is like that of very early to late Yeats, or that of Rupert Brooke to Wallace Stevens. The short poems of the 1925 *Priapus* are necessary exercises in the direction of a new poetic view. Like his *Punch*, Aiken had long seemed to want to give his very profound vision of basic terrors and beauties the trappings and baggage of an elaborate costuming and mannerism. Here he is experimenting with the vision quietly, "alone and unafraid."

The supports of his new point of view are the human consciousness, the imagination, an unceasing experiment with the meanings of words and forms, the superintending chaos of the dark world outside and beyond the room. His essential problem of the Preludes is to reconcile the human consciousness with this chaos, to determine what of each resides in the other, to set up a poetic "frame" in which the fusion may be seen, and to "define." That is, not to define easily, but to move unceasingly toward definition, to offer "preludes to attitude" and "preludes to definition."

II

In her charmingly perceptive note on Aiken's poetry,[6] Marianne Moore speaks of the Memnon of *Preludes for Memnon*[7] as "literally the Amenhotep III colossus at Luxor, cut from a single block of stone, in which a fissure was made by an earth-quake . . ." (*Wake*, 53). The relationship to "The Room" is easily manifest: the monument of craft is invaded by the chaos; and the poet's stance must be taken with respect to both.

Rufus Blanshard correctly says that the two Preludes volumes "must be the central exhibit in the demonstration that Aiken is a major poet" ("Pilgrim's Progress," 140). The word *major* as used here comprises an interaction of intellectual depth and technical skill. In his essay on *Three Philosophical Poets* (fin-ished in 1910, while Aiken was still at Harvard), George San-tayana says that ". . . poetry cannot be spread upon things like butter; it must play upon them like light, and be the medium through which we see them."[8]

I intend the three quotations from these varied sources to stand as introduction to Aiken's "major phase." In a sense, San-tayana is Aiken's type of philosophical critic. The balance of their aesthetic preoccupations is remarkably fine. But, in addi-tion, Aiken is a poet turned to philosophy without ceasing to be a poet—Santayana, a philosopher who turned occasionally to poetry. The light in Aiken's Preludes plays upon "things" and is "the medium through which we see them."

The position of *Preludes for Memnon* is that of an observer who looks both within and beyond himself, and who speculates upon the relationship of the "within" and the "beyond." "Winter for a moment takes the mind; . . ." and the first Prelude begins in a survey of the winter of both. The mind, too, "has its snows, its slippery paths, / Walls bayonetted with ice, leaves ice-encased" (*CP*, 498). The figure of the room as the interior of consciousness is carried over from Senlin and "The Room." Time plays erosively upon the substance of things. Time is a case for enclosing the mind comfortably—like the warmth of a fireplace. But it explodes in the mind, and open a wide abyss into eternity.

> And then the uprush of angelic wings, the beating
> Of wings demonic, from the abyss of the mind:
> (CP, 498-99)

Aiken surveys the particulars of a confused and apparently meaningless life. These are "the bickerings of the inconsequen-tial, / The chatterings of the ridiculous, the iterations / Of the meaningless. . . ." It is the mind's play upon things that opens the way to their being "precious," worthy of attention. It is a desperate affair of devotion in the face of extinction. The mind, addressing itself to phenomena, *becomes* phenomena; or at least it responsibly shares in the ambiguities residing in them.

> And you, because you think of these, are both
> Frost and flower, the bright ambiguous syllable
> Of which the meaning is both no and yes.
>
> (*CP*, 499)

The second Prelude defines "adventure" as evasion. The ceremonies of life (reading, travel, the "trust" in art) overlay the fact of death but do not conceal it.

> And I may be, before our consummation
> Beds us together, cheek by jowl, in earth,
> Swept to another shore, where my white bones
> Will lie unhonored, or defiled by gulls.
>
> (*CP*, 500)

There is nothing here of the religious ecstasy of part two of Eliot's *Ash-Wednesday;* there is only stark recognition of the fact of death. The flesh disintegrates; the bones are not purified in their unfleshing. The gaiety of pleasures remembered quickly dissipates, but there are no easy, compensating joys.

In the dream the reality is grotesquely renewed.[9]

> . . . And I descend
> By a green cliff that fronts the worldlong sea;
> Disastrous shore; where bones of ships and rocks
> Are mixed; and beating waves bring in the sails
> Of unskilled mariners, ill-starred. . . .
>
> (*CP*, 501)

Aiken sees this disaster alleviated in tones, forms—but not really comprehended by them if the poet merely hides in them from it. He captures a delight suddenly, as when "a music" seems to come directly from the dark reaches of chaos; but this is "A seed of fire, fallen in a tinder world" (*CP*, 502). The "brightness of the ineffable" challenges and does not comfort.

It comes down (in Prelude V) to ". . . that seeking for the ding-an-sich, / The feeling itself, the round bright dark emotion" (*CP*, 503). So the problem of reality is an aesthetic one after all: how to make a symbolism stay? But what is a symbol? Perhaps all sharply illuminating experiences are symbolic? But they still "leave the silver core uneaten; / . . . and the whirling You unknown" (*CP*, 503). It is tempting to believe that the words, phrases, conceptions, metaphors are the "You"; or to assume that a constant, loving attention to things will somehow fix "You," make "You" immortal. But poetic form is an act of constantly remaking. Forms are not enduring; even the colossus of Memnon has been cracked by earthquake.

Let us praise nature, chant in an orgy of the sun. This heaven "Of leaves, which rain has loosened from its twig" is after all a charming sight; does it not capture meaning?—"Orion in a cobweb, and the World. . . ." Or, let us depend upon mind: "Conceive: be fecundated by the word." But what are *you*? "A seed, a leaf? a singing congregation / Of molecules? an atom split in two?" (*CP*, 506).

The illusoriness of our conceptual powers is revealed again and again. Self-knowledge, as Festus has told us, is pleasant, and the art of referring knowledge to the self an agreeable interlude. But the mind is the sensations and the knowledges that it has, and these are not fixed. The consciousness flows, and sees its flowing.

> You are all things, and nothing. Ah poor being,
> Sad ghost of wind, dead leaf of autumnal God,
> Bright seed of brief disaster, changing shape:
> (*CP*, 507)

Are there not degrees and gradations of being and nothingness? Does not the rock defy time?

> It is between ourselves these waters flow.
> It is ourselves who are these self-same rocks,—
> (*CP*, 509)

The cry for permanence is a natural cry: it was "old Adam's cry; it was the cry / of human flesh, delivered out of time, / Untimely ripped from chaos; . . ." (*CP*, 510). It leads to anthropomorphic adventures; the investment of faith in a chaos idealized by the desiring mind is a major illusion. Did man create the world, or the world man? It is perhaps better to believe the first; at least, man endures one risk of disaster after another, and—having come "From nightlong dark digestion of the things / He trapped from the chaos of the yesterday"—he endures beyond the necessities of the day.

The thought of destruction persists; death superintends all things living. Our lives are chaoses, touching momentarily. "Your chaos is my world; perhaps my chaos / Is world enough for you . . ." (*CP*, 513). We skirt the edges, constantly, of extinction; the experience of the unknown is impossible to define, except in terms of the known. The basic "known" is the self: it is to that that man returns, "And that is God. It is the seed of seeds: / Seed for disastrous and immortal worlds."

The concluding line of Prelude XIV contains a significant paradox: the self is "the answer that no question asked." It posits the self as focal existence. But existence must be more than known; it must "survive" death, *be* "the answer," the metaphysical reply to all questions. Once again, the idea of self opens the way to infinite speculation about the "particulars of consciousness." This "iridescence, this coruscation, this twinkle—/ This lizard's eye, this fly's wing—!" The self is therefore not the seer only, but the thing seen. The two collaborate in their tense relationships, but they require a way of statement: "Give me a language that will say this thing."

The "thing" itself "is music" because the conscious self—the "I"—has "made music" in the saying of it. He is the "maker" of this thing, which would not be itself were it not that he "made" it in my song.[10]

> It is a sound of many instruments—
> Complex, diverse, an alchemy of voices—
> Brass melting into silver, silver smoothly
> Dissolving into gold; and then the harsh
> And thickening discord: as if chaos yawned
> Suddenly and magnificently for a forest;
>
> (*CP*, 517)

This is the imagination as shaping spirit, but with a difference. The imagination does not simply "admit things" on the way to transforming them. There is no spiritual transcendence, but only an acceptance of the facts: that things exist, that "I" exist, that

"I" can "make song" which heightens the existences of things from which "I" make it; that both things and "I" who "make them" in this sense belong to a chaos from which all emerges, to which all returns.

The familiar image of the mirror (of Prelude XVII) is a convenient illustration. Narcissus (or Senlin, or Forslin, or I) looks at his mirror, admires what he sees, expresses "God's pity" that what he sees cannot endure, then receives his metaphysical "comeuppance."

> . . . A shape he saw
> Unknown before,—obscene, disastrous, huge,—
> Huge as the world, and formless. . . Who this he?
> This dumb, tumultuous, all-including horror?

The figure of Narcissus is changed; the new knowledge shocked him, and "with the mirror dropped, / Wore a new face: such brightness and such darkness, / Pitiless, as a moonblanched desert wears" (*CP*, 519). The challenge, perhaps not here accepted by the Narcissus-fool, is to *see* oneself within the chaos, creating the forms that exist on the other side. Further, the self needs to accept "all the tumults in this action" (*CP*, 520): the wars of atoms, the disappearance of graceful things that are in and yet not in the range of consciousness. It watches a parade of things, a procession of dark shades upon wide water.

> . . . The bird is gone:
> And while you wait, another comes and goes,—
> Another and another; yet your eye,
> Although it has not moved, can scarcely say
> If birds have come and gone . . .
>
> (*CP*, 521)

It is a false succession, but the marks of time make up an eternity, the only eternity the self may comprehend. The self is constantly threatened by its flux, and the flux is itself the challenge to the self. It must plunge "From time's colossal brink into that chasm / Of change and limbo and immortal flux . . ." (*CP*, 523). Both phenomena take shape and pass away. The mind changes as the shapes of things float and pass away. "Permanence" is an accretion of changes—"the flowing / Of shape to shape which means all shapelessness."

Prelude XXIV portrays the self as a "magnificent angel" poised in "the pure aether of a thought," the unconscious beating "the words of nescience" (*CP*, 527) and sustaining knowledge. This instant of knowing is what the self knows of eternity: but how can it name it? The instrument of knowing is the word, which the self at first clumsily, hesitantly grasps, which slowly takes shape: ". . . a syllable, / Meaningless in itself, which lights a word;"

> The pause, between two words, which makes a meaning;
> The gulf between two stones which make a world.
>
> (*CP*, 528)

This metaphor is an important phase in Aiken's preludes to "attitude"; it is significant that the "syllable" appears as a pause between words, as a space between objects; that "word" and "world" are here interrelated. The process is reciprocal, inter-active, compensatory. Meaning is thing, but it is also the pause between things, between the "adventures" of perceptions which bring things to consciousness. This relationship is necessary if the curiously balanced interchange between observer and ob-served is to be maintained.

The "truth" is otherwise somehow illusory, "a sum of surds" (*CP*, 529). We *are* the truth; the pulse of it enters the pulse of the universe. Aiken moves steadily, though with an infinite slow-ness, toward it. He is not "laying down the law," nor reading the law already laid out. He cannot deify the mind, nor reify God. But he can move steadily toward definition and attitude.

The Preludes are quiet; they do not gesture or rave or rant. They describe a painful and a painstaking progress, though it is often not a "progress" at all, but rather a series of tentative sug-gestions, withdrawn, to be called on again when the context for them is ready. This is the true kind of "symphonic" movement; the substance of it is not echoes and repetitions of sound, but minuscule variations of the word, the consciousness—movements toward a "suitable metaphor."

There are two major questions toward which these poems maneuver in search—not of answer, but of attitude: time and consciousness. The observer notes the specificity of time, in clocks and calendars, in the "mid-waste of life"; but time is an-other thing as well.

What is time, the clock says what is time,
Never the past, never the future, always the now,
(CP, 533)

The succession of moments is what we are; but we are qualitatively what our consciousnesses have made of them. How are we to distinguish between "idiot trifles" (CP, 534) and "the sunrise on the grass-blade" (CP, 535)? It is a matter of emotional economy: disorders and "the hothead factions of the soul" (CP, 536) held in balance. The mastery of chaos comes from a creative knowing: "The quick brief cry of memory, that knows / At the dark's edge how great the darkness is" (CP, 539).

The Preludes are a play upon these ideas. They do not arrive at, they are always a moving toward, definition. They exist, like the composition that has not been finished, but which we, who are composers, too, can finish. We have the means, are born with the words, at first not our words, but those of others. We must sweep away these words (or these specific or local meanings) and "from our anger, / Our pride, our bitterness, our sweetness too, / And what our kidneys say, and what our hearts" (CP, 541), make our own language.

We cannot think evil because "it has been thought," but we must "Go back again, and find the divine dark" (CP, 543). This requirement involves an annotation of nature, of experiences, captured within the time of experiencing them.

Then say: I was a part of nature's plan;
Knew her cold heart, for I was consciousness;
Came first to hate her, and at last to bless;
(CP, 548)

Perhaps the most important statement in *Preludes for Memnon* occurs in XLV. It suggests the intimate and the terrible interrelationships which the Preludes have been trying to annotate.

I have read
Time in the rock and in the human heart,
Space in the bloodstream, and those lesser works
Written by rose and windflower on the summer, sung
By water and snow, deciphered by the eye,
Translated by the slaves of memory,
And all that you be you, and I be I,
Or all that by imagination, aping

> God, the supreme poet of despair,
> I may be you, you me, before our time
> Knowing the rank intolerable taste of death,
> And walking dead on the still living earth.
>
> (*CP*, 551-52)

Probably an oversimplification, this statement does come as close to the stance Aiken wishes to take as any expressed in his lines. The rock and the bloodstream, physically antithetic, are in this economy comparable measures of existence. The memory brings impressions together, but it is through communication of the "I" and the "you" that they have any chance at all of surviving as more than impressions. Most important, there is an identity of the bloodstream and the rock, and this relationship has been remarked before. The close resemblances of living matter help to defeat annihilation and prepare the way to definition.

R. P. Blackmur has said that the Preludes "present the actual predicaments of the enacting consciousness with the minimum resort to formula and the maximum approach to form. . . ."[11] Aiken has deliberately ruled out formula, while he seemed often in earlier works to search anxiously for it before he was willing to commit himself. He has not entirely succeeded in *Preludes for Memnon*. There are some clichés that still cling to the presentation. Jesus, Judas, Blake, Shakespeare, and others still intrude. They are not made use of; they simply stand there in the line, in the way.

For the most part, however, Aiken is about his business of presenting "the actual predicament of the enacting consciousness." The following lines are an example of how his allusiveness, unlike Eliot's, is likely to handicap the progress of what he wants to say:

> Jesus is not the spokesman of the Lord:
> Confucius neither, nor Nietzsche, no, nor Blake;
> But you yourself. Hold out your hand, and stare
> At fingers, palm and fingernails, the wrist
> Supple and strong, and wonder whence it comes,
> And what its purpose is.
>
> (*CP*, 556)

The first two lines have nothing to do with the case, the next four everything; but they are spoiled by the reflection of tone from the beginning. Ultimately the idea, which in other Preludes comes through freely, is in this case close to being a platitude.

There are unprofitable echoes as well, as in LIII: "For god's sake let us sit on honest ground / And tell harsh stories of the deaths of kings!" (*CP*, 561). The figures of Verlaine and Rimbaud of LVI do not entirely share this fault. They are clearly realized, independently of their associations with "the great" and the "soulful." In fact, whatever echoes of the men in the names the lines have, usually help the idea along. The principal use of these two is the verse of Verlaine, "Prends l'éloquence et tords-lui son cou!" of "Art Poétique," which is echoed here: "We must take rhetoric and wring its neck! . . ."

This idea is developed some lines later, when Aiken takes up its implications:

> Let us describe the evening as it is:—
> The stars disposed in heaven as they are:
> Verlaine and Shakspere rotting, where they rot,
> Rimbaud remembered, and too soon forgot;
>
> Order in all things, logic in the dark;
> Arrangement in the atom and the spark;
> Time in the heart and sequence in the brain—
>
> Such as destroyed Rimbaud and fooled Verlaine.
> And let us then take godhead by the neck—
>
> And strangle it, and with it, rhetoric.
>
> (*CP*, 565)

The central situation of the Preludes is better presented in LXI; in it the struggle against mortality is graphically and originally communicated. Do we need to resort to sentimentality, the poet asks. Do we need "Imaginary gods to pity us"?

> Saying
> We are unworthy, father, to be remembered,
> We are unworthy to be remembered, mother,
> Remember us, O clods from whom we come—
> (*CP*, 569)

Nevertheless, the ideas of the Preludes are here too rhetorically stressed, and this especially in the poem's concluding lines.

> . . . What we remember,
> Why that's ourselves; and if ourselves be honest,
> We'll know this world of straws and leaves and hearts
> Too well to give it power.
>
> (*CP*, 570)

Preludes for Memnon ends very quietly, rather like the concluding "prayer" of "Changing Mind." The conceit is that of
Eliot's *Burnt Norton*, Part II, with its "trilling wire in the blood,"
the "dance along the artery," and "the circulation of the lymph,"[12]
which are repeated in:

> Thus systole addressed diastole,—
> The heart contracting, with its grief of burden,
> To the lax heart, with grief of burden gone.
>
> (*CP*, 572)

Aiken does not, however, resolve the problem of these ambiguities. Having already strangled both godhead and rhetoric,
he must close in this indecisive way:

> No language leaps this chasm like a lightning:
> Here is no message of assuagement, blown
> From Ecuador to Greenland: here is only
>
> A trumpet blast, that calls dead men to arms;
> The granite's pity for the cloud; the whisper
> Of time to space.
>
> (*CP*, 573)

III

Whatever is imperfectly realized in *Preludes for Memnon* is left
to *Time in the Rock* to complete.[13] Here, in the ninety-six "*Preludes to Definition*," Aiken gives us what is undoubtedly his
greatest work. There are individual short lyrics in other volumes
that are as good in their own way, but no sustained long work.
We may be prejudiced in favor of *Time in the Rock* because it
pays so much attention to the problems of language; it offers
an *ars poetica* that should delight any critic. But its virtues
surely go beyond that matter. The major philosophical theme
which Aiken has sensed throughout his career—and had more
than begun to define in *Preludes to Memnon*—is here elaborated
upon with a subtlety and an integrity that are rare indeed. In

Preludes for Memnon he was seen, rather melodramatically at times, dispensing with the godhead. In *Time in the Rock* he takes up the implications of a dismissed godhead, the great secular responsibilities of consciousness. As Rufus Blanshard has said ("Pilgrim's Progress," 145), "Poetry is therefore a religious act."

Time in the Rock takes up where *Preludes for Memnon* had stopped—in a sense, where it had failed. Aiken's statement in *Rock* is indeed sparse and relentless. The human consciousness is immediately implicated in an unresolved issue. The fury of chaos is picked up as a series of negations that are not quite negations, but are left for the consciousness to grasp.

> And there I saw the seed upon the mountain
> but it was not a seed it was a star
> but it was not a star it was a world
> but it was not a world it was a god
> but it was not a god it was a laughter

The arteries are roots, the roots arteries; the two are identifiably one, and both partake in and are responsible for the destructive forces of the world. It is not the fact of this identity, but the fact that it is seen, comprehended, by the mind: "and thus beneath the web of mind I saw" (*Rock*, 1).

This, then, is "our theme," if that is what we need: the fact that we need a theme, a principle to guide us in this chaos, perhaps protects us from it. We learn to live by accepting death. This is an act not customary to those who formulate the principles, or judge the balances, in nature. The "angels" of high thought and the humble sentient beings are not unlike one another. The simple integrities will grow strong wings, will become majestic with their insights, and dare to replace the "bright angels" who occupy the outer spaces (*Rock*, 4). We must follow the pattern to where it disappears, "reduce the granite downward, to no stone: / unhinge the rainbow to his sun and rain . . ." (*Rock*, 6), and thus "to wisdom bring / terror from terror, and the thing from thing" (*Rock*, 7).

The basic problem, as of *Preludes for Memnon,* is to bring the word and the wound together. How does the "salty syllable" relate? What is "True inwardness"? The consciousness is dissolved, resolved, dissolved again, "dispersed in some such terms, phrased, rephrased" (*Rock,* 13). Let us have no fantasies, creeds, "no dead gods hung on crosses in a shop" (*Rock,* 14). Let it rather be the intimate substance of the world that challenges and substantiates and modifies our search and discovery:

> let it be self displacing self
> as quietly as a child lifts a pebble,
> as softly as a flower decides to fall,—
> self replacing self
> as seed follows flower to earth.
>
> (*Rock,* 15)

The trouble is language, the "idiot words," to find the word, the syllable, that is you. This act encloses the wound that is reality, checks the madness that is awareness of it.

> Be then of madness all compact—
> singular soul whose word is act
> Singular act whose word is sole
> embassy of angelic whole—!
>
> (*Rock,* 20)

Time, matter, and the viscous substance of reality are all a part of the wound, which the word must heal. There is the fact of the "dreadful commonplace," in which nothing happens while everything is, the "immortal worm / under the table and beneath the world, / working his comic passage toward death" (*Rock,* 23). Aiken kneads emotions into the substance of the world, so that the identity of consciousness with it has tonal values as well as challenges to knowing. The roots of the tree suffer agony and urge "their grief against the dark, waiting, / and yet not waiting, for inconceivable rest" (*Rock,* 25).

To this conception Aiken adds the major one of the self's seeking selfhood, moving toward definition: "a world of selves trying to remember the self / before the idea of self is lost—" (*Rock,* 28). That "angel of bright consciousness," man, assumes an awful risk—not only of not achieving his aim of self-knowledge, but of being destroyed.

In XXII, Aiken suggests man as consciousness, woman as the unconscious, and the child as "that frail mirror of the sky." All three of them venture forth, pause "in the simple light," and return to the "house of evening," the hall which is the room and its encompassing universal chaos (*Rock*, 32-33). It is in one sense a terrifying conceit, but it also suggests courage, perhaps more properly a vital innocence, before the terrors of uninformed and unordered matter.

The poet must find the voice for all this. Is one voice like another, as good as another? Is there no discrimination to be found among voices? Or, is it a matter of voices or of syllables? *Preludes for Memnon* had put the case for the syllable's being the space between rocks, the pause between instants. In *Rock* Aiken invests syllables with the heavy pressures of both emotional tone and causes: "the heavy syllables of doubt, or of despair— / speaking passionately, speaking bitterly, hunger or hope / ordering the words, that are like sounds of flame—" (*Rock*, 35).

The picture world is not enough; it falls apart. The colors we admired in childhood, the passions of dark and light, are swallowed by time. They are too closely associated with promises, which time has blotted out, or will blot out. We must see, "to know the terror of seeing"; be, "to know the terror of being"; know, "to know the dreadfulness of knowledge" (*Rock*, 39). How can we sum up the world, lift it from the sand-grains that are its fragmentary parts? The only source of knowledge is language, "the unending glossary of the world" (*Rock*, 40).

In XXVII, Aiken reviews the performers who have tried to imitate the gestures and curves and volutions of the world: the mountebank, "this leaper / of mortal benches, and immortal hoops"; the priest, who "if bitterness makes the healing word, / sells crucifixes to the crucified"; the soothsayer, reader of fortunes, conveyor of easy magic. He replaces them with the commonplace man:

> is he not perfect, walks he not divinely
> with a light step among the stars his fathers
> with a quick thought among the seeds his sons.
> (*CP*, 42)

For it is true that not the word alone, or the gesture and the word, bespeak reality; it is the pressure both put upon the object to meet its own passionate pressure. The word comes hard, if it is genuine. The speaker is "only a summary of that world"; he cannot communicate authority because it is he who speaks. It is a matter of the word's being a "summary of force," of pressures, physical and natural, interiorities yielding to externals (*Rock*, 44-45). The god speaks out of "the blind almighty hard" (*Rock*, 47); and each act has a voice, if it will find words.

> But let us praise the voice the lonely voice
> but let us praise the leaf that is the first
> but let us praise the syllable the only
> that syllable which is the seed of worlds.
>
> (*Rock*, 49)

The obligation to know follows upon the obligation to experience: first the fragments of the quotidian, then the forms, then "that vaster form which moves / along the beaches of a vaster ocean, / the naked shape of an unwilling will" (*Rock*, 53). One cannot merely store up speech against the demon; for speech is itself the demon, or part of it. The self must dismiss the attractive notion that words "get in the way of reality" and will protect him from it.

All light, darkness, cold, heat, brightness, depth, have "words." Aiken takes as illustration the mind of the child who first seeks out cries that are not even words to identify himself. He has a partial language, the language of innocence; but he must submit to the terrors of experience, develop a language of this terror, clarify this relationship to it, be on the alert against its losing its power to put pressure on reality.

> In the clear shaft of light the man so standing
> alone, but his aloneness known,
> all things accepting, all things gladly heeding,
> the heart beating, the hand bleeding,
> the lost world now again his own
> and marvellous with understanding.
>
> (*Rock*, 63)

Here is a midpoint on the way to definition: the "aloneness known" is a quiet restatement of the melodramatic strangling of the godhead. The lines also define the several stages of the journey: the lost innocence recaptured through acceptance of its complexity, understanding achieved through an unceasing participation in being-knowing, finally the language of the knowing: "Who would carve words must carve himself / first carve himself—" (*Rock*, 64).

Language is easily an agent of deception, an ornamental false-hood. It is, first of all, falsely arbitrary, wearisomely logical ("A leads to b and b to c . . . ," (*Rock*, 68). But if we find speech for "what without speech we knew and could not say," (*Rock*, 69) we should be shortly on our way. A tough consciousness will serve:

> Surround the thing with phrases, and perceptions;
> master it with all that muscle gives
> of mastery to mind,—all strengths, all graces,
> flexes and hardnesses; the hand, the foot;
> quick touch of delight, recoil of disgust;
> (*Rock*, 71)

A total absorption of the thing is a minimal requisite, "the whole body is wisdom, the whole body's cunning . . ." (*Rock*, 72). The mind's soliloquy is repeated in the wind's, "the drowning one balanced breathless in the wind" (*Rock*, 73).

The true hero of the modern world, as Aiken sees him, is the unsentimental "I," the person who says "I" when evidence demeans or threatens his self-confidence. He is the completely existential hero who will look quite unblinkingly into the abyss of his world, note the ambiguities of our evasive attempts to hide from it, and use words as rough-hewn and as sharply hewn as they can be fashioned.

He lives not by *politesse*, but candidly and openly, freely submitting to negation in the knowledge that he creates negation as he creates himself. In other words, he must make a virtue of enduring what Professor Beach has called the "moral terror" of a secular world. Perhaps his hardest trial is to find a multiform truth practicable, to find a balance among truths:

> . . . Here's the division
> between one truth and other which is false
> between one lie and other which is true
> between one hour and other which is nothing
> between one eye and other which is hell.
> (*Rock*, 83)

It is a test of knowing, of "noticing." How often, Aiken asks, do we find ourselves attentive to the particulars of our immediate experiencing? The shadow on the white wall, the imprint

of pencil on paper, the waves' design and the waves' ghost, the
path of the wind in a field of wheat: "Notice how little, and how
seldom, you notice / the movement of the eyes in your own face,
reflection / of a moment's reflection . . ." (*Rock*, 87).

Beyond these, what of the emotional pressures, the heart's
pushing against desires, suffering change and rebuke? And the
will: "and how does it come / this wave of the will how does
it enter the blood / that thus with your hand you feel it and
clutch it"? (*Rock*, 89). It is easy to find ready answers to cover
up the full meaning of questions: the true existential terror is
the terror of nothingness, the zero that exists beyond the seeing
self. This design is "the tombstone of the usual one" (*Rock*, 91),
but it must become like the unusual. Formality or informality
is a matter of the cast of experience; it cannot be imposed. The
skeleton has its own formality; it can parade, or dance the dance
of death: "Let it observe its exquisite decorum / in the manipulation of decay—" (*Rock*, 94).

Poem LXVII gives us the image of the man on the stage of
his "own imagining"; the percipient ego creates what he sees,
like the actor of Stevens' "Of Modern Poetry": "speak to the
large bright imaginary audience / that flattering multiplication
of yourself. . . ." It is a vital challenge, one almost never met.
For man is too easily tempted to confide falsehoods: ". . . to be
supercilious to one's self / even in one's dramatic moments!—
marvellous / decay of what in God's first declaration / might
have been good" (*Rock*, 97).

This demonstration of the existentialist's *"mauvaise foi"* is ir-
revocable, or almost so. For the word "walks with us, is a ghost
of word" (*Rock*, 98). Far worse is the challenge to say that we
are nothing, and expect to be nothing, to "accept my worship
Zero for these devotions" (*Rock*, 99):

> (It is here that the little doubt comes in from the window
> like a cold wind fluttering the leaves
> and we ourselves go forth again on that wind
> to become Lord Zero.)
>
> (*Rock*, 100)

The calamity of inner understanding involves our being aware
that calamity is itself a "pressure word" that means nothing
because the universe is indifferent to its emotional implications.

Destiny is indifferent equally to successes and defeats. We are not victims of it, or lucky inheritors of it, but recipients; it "happens to us," as we happen to it. To make aesthetic patterns from this happenstance requires an act of courage, or perhaps an act of supreme innocence—as in the child's joy of LXXIV (*Rock*, 104-5). The act of the conscious observer (see LXXVIII, 110-11), penetrates beyond what is seen in the order of words on a book, or beyond the lines of the shapes in a room, is a performance of the utmost integrity.

> God
> is such a margin as thus lies between
> the poem and the page's edge, a space
> between the known and the imagined, between
> the reported and the real. He is your fancy.
> And you are his.
>
> (*Rock*, 111)

This is as close to being "pure Stevens" as anything Aiken has ever written; and I have remarked several times about the similarities of the two poets. R. P. Blackmur reviews *Time in the Rock* along with Stevens' *Owl's Clover*,[14] and he finds them both moving in the direction of great reflective poetry. The comparison is justified, at least in terms of the above passage. God is "a supreme fiction" here; there is an interchange of creative fancy; the imagination intervenes in the processes of reality; and the truth lies somewhere "between the known and the imagined." But such a passage as this is comparatively rare in Aiken's poetry, which is also much more morally demanding than Stevens'. That is, Aiken does not perform the act of the supreme fiction usually, but merely suggests its necessity. He goes on to other matters, focusing on the observer and upon the peculiarities of his discovering absences and voids, which stand in the way of teleological assurance.

Here, however, he is transported by an "innocent joy," to find that meanness supports beauty, or does not prevent it. In LXXIX, he points in delight to the lustre, light, with which the daybreak "strikes the bronzed cobweb, so that it quickens to gold," and he begs the observer to hold to it as "a proof of your love" (*Rock*, 112). This emphasis is a part of the task of clearing the way of bombast—melodramatic readings of nature—which bars the way to simple pleasures.

Assurance, he says, "can come from nothing, or almost nothing" (*Rock*, 114). The pattern of waves upon the shore, for example, reveals much that is simple, something intricate, but above all a suggestion of what lies beyond both.

> . . . The long waves come
> to drown their fading rims of foam in sand
> white arcs on intersected arcs of white
> with all their sound, and all their power; you see
> the wilderness; and in the face of this
> your poem becomes the perfect shape it is;
> the sea left out!
> And thus, you know the world.
> Thus, with a phrase, exclude the absolute.
> (*Rock*, 116-17)

One does not "make" the sea; nor does the sea "make" the poem. The poem is a joint effort—the result of an effort (much more so than in the case of Stevens' artist) to "submit" to the sea's force, daring, and grace.

The struggle with nothingness is unceasing. Each understanding in art or gesture or mere reconciliation is a temporary halt at best—until it is discovered that the act of poetry and the act of life are the same: the poem being a compromise, as be tween two converging brutalities.

> . . . Destiny leans above us
> like nothing: we know nothing: how can we say
> therefore that it leans? it is not an old man,
> nor a young one, wears no clothes, and reads no book,
> nor delivers lectures; . . .
> (*Rock*, 124)

Again and again, Aiken approaches definition, all but grasps it, sets it aside (as being not definition but a suggestive glimpse of it), and begins the process once again. There is no "development" in any elementary sense. Yet the Preludes of *Time in the Rock* fill the mind as a slow stream of water fills a large space. The instances do more than merely accumulate; we are not after a sum, but after many ways of envisioning a central, archetypal situation.

Poem LXXXIX is an excellent illustration of the process. The changes in nature reflect in changes in the self. Yet beyond these, there are the "invisible" and the "unspoken," which are linked to death and are at least forms of farewell. Consciousness dies, or seems to; but it also survives, or seems to. The voyage into the "gulf between / bellsound and waiting and bellsound and then / the unfilled silence which sets a term to time . . ." (*Rock*, 129).

The process is renewed, until it becomes itself (consciousness ceases, death takes over). The self takes what it gives—even in death, for the image of courage or the image of weakness remains: "Greatly your own greatness the net brings back; / or, weakly dared and flung, your own soul's lack" (*Rock*, 132). The book closes on a note of the simple (yet bold, and intricate) joining of selves.

> Self, and other self—permit them, permit them—
> it is summer still, winter can do no more
> who brings them together in death, let them come
> murderously now together, it is the lifelong
> season of meeting, speak your secret.
>
> (*Rock*, 138)

The two volumes of Aiken's maturity show a marvel of growth. Perhaps it is the act of trimming irrelevancies from a field of discourse long since known that makes them so. Perhaps, also, Aiken has wearied of inventing aesthetic poses which drain away the initiative of knowing. The Preludes are not barren; they are the opposite of empty. But their richness is not that of a riot of lines and tones, a manipulation of "emotion-tones," but a graceful balancing of form against the processes of thought he is describing. He is more than ever the speculative poet, the reflective poet; but he seldom needs to wave the arms of rhetoric to attract the attention of the mind which follows him.

The "substance" of the Preludes is the act of approaching definition, of coming to an end of questioning. Perhaps the best way to describe it is to say that in human experience the *answer* to any basic question appears abruptly, brutally, unexpectedly, and, in a limited sense, tragically. The poet's task is to find the intricacies and subtleties of the questions to which the answer relates.

The excellence of the poems is also in their forms, for there is seldom any doubt about their appropriateness. If we object to the absence of individualization, we find the same lack in Stevens' *Notes Toward a Supreme Fiction*.[15] The truth is that the specifics lie in the language and the lines. The results are tonally the exact opposite of those in most of the "Symphonies," where the reader is constantly distracted by side-shows. We have the feeling that the ambiguities are intrinsic and necessary —and that, if we follow through on them, we will reach a point where they will be not resolved but assimilated.

CHAPTER *6*

The Man of Letters

I

BETWEEN the two volumes of Preludes and after them, Conrad Aiken published nine volumes of original poetry,[1] two of them in the years 1931 to 1936: *The Coming Forth by Day of Osiris Jones*[2] and *Landscape West of Eden.*[3] These are both in the mode of earlier works, dramatic rather than expository statements, and in some ways *tours de force.* The manner is perhaps more restrained, the plans less ambitious, than those of the "Symphonies." *Osiris Jones* is in the nature of a modern version of the ancient funerary roll of grave-book. Aiken acknowledges indebtedness to E. A. Wallis Budge's British Museum pamphlet containing translations from *The Book of the Dead.*

For Osiris Jones (as for his better known namesake) the record is a test of his guilt or innocence; it also answers the question of what manner of man he was in his lifetime.[4] The poem remains faithful to the details of its model. Only the arrangement of them is interesting. We have seen enough of the kind of "meaning" ascribed to them, in *Senlin* especially, to know what form that will take. *Osiris Jones* is an inventory of things, sayings, books, and acts. Of course there are no gods to whom this inventory will actually be submitted; Jones's life is, after all, of no account, except the account that might be made of the "commonplace man." Both ordinary men and kings go to rest; an indifferent grass grows on all graves.

> Little is life, with love, or without love,
> with or without wings, bones can scarcely move,
> rain will destroy the flesh, the eyes go blind,
> and stone will not remember much the mind.
>
> (*Osiris Jones,* 11)

The value of *Osiris Jones* depends entirely on accepting its frame, its idea. Without interest in that, the verse is scarcely worth the try. Once again, Aiken has come up with a device: cleverly, ingeniously, partially effective. The testing or weighing of an ordinary man's life, as against those of kings or gods, has a rudimentary ironic value. But the device is a distraction.

Landscape West of Eden has much of the same quality: the use of an ancient religious myth for the purpose of discussing modern issues. In it is a fantasy of the Garden, seen through a god's eye, and concerned with the desire, or curiosity, of Adam and Eve with respect to the world beyond. It is a landscape *West* of Eden that tempts; and the poem may be thought of as a commentary upon the westernizing of human ambitions. Adam wishes to make the move out of Eden: is it not possible that there is a land beyond, even more delightful than this? If it is evil, he can always escape it, and return. Eden is itself portrayed as a symbol of static perfection; Adam is lured by the thought of change.

The Fall as pictured by Aiken is change as opposed to a fixed world. "If thought must change, as changing seasons change, / change to the dictates of the blood and moon, the mind / moving to measures of the mere unmeaning—" (*Eden,* 27-28): if this be true, the god says, then how shall we determine truth of action and movement? Do we need to know the unknown? Should we not be satisfied with what is perfectly clear, within Edenic limits? But, says Adam, Eden is our childhood; are we to remain children forever? (*Eden,* 37). The poem concludes with the god-narrator looking out at the future, the West, disturbed over what is to come.

> I trembled with the beginnings of this new power;
> already half-distinct I saw that fevered world;
> inchoate lewdnesses becoming shapes,
> shadows becoming lurid delicious lights,
> all whirling, mad, and with delirium's wonder,
> splendours of foulness. . . .
>
> (*Eden,* 40)

Landscape West of Eden offers a familiar symbol of the absolute, as against change. The god's fear is not only of change but of another absolute, that of "unmeaning." In any case, he is mostly on the defensive. The fact of static creation has no place in Aiken's thought. The movement is down and away— West, not only because West is the direction of our civilization, the challenge to our ambitions and our principles (it is also the American challenge),[5] but also because it is the direction of the setting sun. Decline, decay, the breaks in the frame of perfection, all lie there.

Here it is Adam and not Eve who wishes to yield to the temptation; Eve, who prefers the established fixities, does not want to take the risks. Taking the poem beyond its setting, one may assume it to be a model of its kind of discussion: the choice of settling for "fixities" or of risking the uncertainties of change. Both *Osiris Jones* and *Eden* offer interesting conceptions; both distract by the weight of their allusiveness. The entire conception of each depends for its success upon our "going the whole way" in accepting the pattern and the paraphernalia of its initial assumptions. In the end, what comes through is so relatively simple it scarcely encourages analysis.

II

In 1940 Aiken published a sequence of forty-three sonnets called *And in the Human Heart*.[6] They are a working out in another form of the thoughts of the Preludes. Statements achieve a more apparently formal quality within the limits of the sonnet; they acquire "dignity" without adding significance. In sonnet VI, for example, the body is an altar; religion gives way to secular concerns.

> This body must my only altar make;
> there will I burn the miracle, and there
> the bread and wine of strict communion take,
>
> .   .   .   .
>
> O *Altitudo* in the bloodstream swims,
> the god of love sings in the very bone.
>   (*CP,* 760)

Both the language and the argument of the Preludes are preserved but limited, perhaps, to conform to the title. The idea of bodily, emotional self-sufficiency involves a looking downward and inward, rather than cosmic adventures. They are "love sonnets" in the sense that the poet's love, "in the human heart," will confine and balance the threats of "all-overarching heaven, fierce dome of azure" (*CP*, XI, 763). The love wills acceptance of death, but it holds to the physical limiting of eternity:

> eternity spreads time-rings in this flower:
> and you, your hands among the blossoms counting,
> are but another time and measure mounting.
>
> > (*CP*, XXI, 768)

There is much reliance upon thought, upon its gaining the initiative over chaos through recognition: "and yet, to think the abyss is to escape it, / or fix that horror's margin in a rhyme;" (*CP*, XXVI, 770). The human heart is held to as center, from which the mind may move outward, to return within. The set limits of the sonnet help to express this centripetal motion.

> Yet inward look as well, where bloodstream beats
> intolerable pain, and therein seek
> islands and kingdoms, source of frosts and heats,
> cancer and chaos; . . .
>
> .   .   .   .
>
> here, too, our balconies, from which to see
> end and beginning, and the star-bearing tree.
>
> > (*CP*, XXXVI, 775)

The conceit of self-containment, self-initiative, is maintained to the end: "all's here that is, or will be, or has been. / Rejoice, my love, our histories begin!" (*CP*, XLIII, 779).

Brownstone Eclogues and Other Poems[7] is in many respects a genuine achievement. Once again, the soul of the city is the subject, but the conception is not inhibited as it was in *The House of Dust*. The first poem, "Sursum Corda" (3-4) is one of the great modern commentaries on the Christ symbol. It is significantly different from echoes of that symbol in the longer poems, for its concentration is upon the human implication (complicity) in the death of Christ.

The idea is not original, of course; it goes back at least to Dostoevsky in modern literature. But the development of it stands superbly well the comparison with contemporary versions.

Aiken views the city as a landscape of pain, self-inflicted, so that the Christ, who has in the past offered his divinity to man, here becomes a victim indistinguishable from his assailant.[8] Ultimately, we are Christ, and the guilt is ours for the evil we have committed.

> Wherever death's red hand unhusks a heart,
> or tiger ice rips the meek hills apart,
> there we lie down alone, and lonely spend
> the spirit's silence to the spirit's end.
>
> (*Eclogues*, 3)

The acceptance of responsibility is communicated in language and metaphor precisely suited to it. Aiken's gift, here admirably controlled, has no better evidence of what it may do.

The "metaphysicals" of brownstone fronts and of the streets that run between them are presented in a variety of other ways. "North Infinity Street" echoes Eliot's "Preludes," but has its own distinctive qualities. There are individual portraits: of the Jewish junk-man and "his quixotic horse" (*Eclogues*, 13); of old "Goody Two-Shoes," at the corner, "the tray of votive shoestrings in her hands" (28). But for the most part, the images define the city less specifically: the dilapidated dignity of past brownstone elegance; the street that "lost its reputation. / They call it now the Alley of Assignation" (*Eclogues*, 41); the street of "All Death, All Love," with the elevated rattling above, rows of slate below (*Eclogues*, 49).

In the volume's longest poem, "Blues for Ruby Matrix," Aiken attempts an apostrophe to the spirit of woman in the city. It recalls Hart Crane's "Faustus and Helen" in some respects, his "Southern Cross"[9] in others. Ruby is the slum princess: "the wretched streets that in-and-out are you, / there where the cry of pain is in the bone," (*Eclogues*, 75). There is not much else to be said for this moderately effective poem, except that it depends rather too much on our being sentimentally given to the slum pathos with which its subject is invested.[10]

The poetry of war is more than ordinarily liable to damaging clichés. Aiken himself, reviewing some World War I poets in *Scepticisms*, pointed to the risks: "What immediately suggests itself is that as war is hideously and predominantly real, an affair of overwhelmingly sinister and ugly forces, it can only be embodied successfully (with exceptions) in an art which is realistic, or psycho-realistic . . ." (222).

There are many uncertainties in *The Soldier*,[11] a long poem of varied rhythms, which tries not so much to describe war as to come to terms with it, the "business of bloodletting, your ancient profession . . ." (7). Through most of the poem, Aiken tries to see the war as a part of the economy of human and natural weakness and brutality. Nature survives it; dying goes on there, seasonally, with or without war (9). There is violence in nature and out. Throughout history, ". . . Life strives with death, / warcraft shall wax in the hero; ever the wise man / ponders the strife of this world" (12).

The Soldier is not a successful poem. It casts no new illuminations either on the problem of violence and sensibility or on Aiken's status as a poet. It was undoubtedly written within too close a range; but it also seems to have been written from ignorance. The figure of the soldier here is like the one who might serve a text in a formal ceremony. Aiken's attempt to write poetry for "occasions," however large these may be, are not distinguished. There are suggestions of the literature of World War I, of MacLeish, and of Dos Passos; there are also echoes of Auden's poems of World War II; finally as in the following lines, Aiken speaks in the voice of Wallace Stevens' *Notes Toward a Supreme Fiction:*

> . . . Look home from the desert, soldier:
> to the regenerate desert of the heart come home:
> and know that this too needs heroes and endurance, and ardor
> *(Soldier,* 31)

The Kid[12] seems at least to have had a happier beginning. The historical basis of the poem is a man named William Blackstone, or Blaxton, who was in possession of Boston Common when the first settlers arrived there. When the place became too "crowded" for him, he settled near what was to become Providence, Rhode Island, where he died in 1675. Aiken wrote of him: "He is a tantalizing figure, in many respects the true prototypical American: ancestor alike of those pioneers who sought freedom and privacy in the 'wide open spaces,' or the physical conquest of an untamed continent, and those others, early and late, who were to struggle for it in the darker kingdoms of the soul . . ." ("Author's Note," *The Kid,* 6).

The poem, a galloping succession of couplets, celebrates the "westernizing" of man. Blackstone becomes a variety of persons to demonstrate the progress of the American personality:

> And westward, seaward, he drew the horizon,
> following the Sioux, who followed the bison,
> westward, along the Missouri no more,
> far back remembered like Ohio's shore,
> far back forgotten like the moosewood tree
> and dust in the mouth on a prairie sea,
> the watergap crossed, the chinquapins gone,
> breast-high laurel, and still heading on.
> *(The Kid,* 11)

The hero assumes the forms of the several early American celebrities: Crèvecoeur, Audubon, Thoreau, Johnny Appleseed, Daniel Boone, and so on: "Westward he rode, and the masks he wore; / southward he rode, and the names he bore" (*The Kid,* 25).

The pattern is that of Aiken's 1937 essay on the "Literature of Massachusetts,"[13] with a handful of Westerners thrown in for good and handsome measure. As in the essay, Aiken brings in Melville's Captain Ahab as the symbol of America's turning its attention to the "cloud of evil": Ahab, searching

> for a god more evil, but to worship more:
> the god of hatred, of bland white evil,
> the world incarnate as a blind white devil:
> *(The Kid,* 30)

The poem concludes in the *personae* of Henry and Brooks Adams, Whitman, and Emily Dickinson; the last marks the end of the premodern American spirit: "And sleeps in the churchyard, unlaureled the stone, / where lies the intrinsic, unknown, and alone" (*The Kid,* 32).

No number of notes and marginal "pointers" can atone for the superficiality of this poem. The conception is faulty, the shifts of terms and of the grounds for action, the almost frivolous slightness with which major, important ideas are treated, all mark *The Kid* as one of Aiken's conspicuous failures.

Some such poem as this is certainly desirable, but it is difficult to achieve. Aiken's seems too much the rhymed essay, with no differentiation of tone; the Kid's identity changes easily, but only his original self seems to have a shadow of authenticity. There is, of course, the unsuitability of the meter—or, perhaps, its monotony. The couplets are too easily a source of motion, at least as Aiken uses them. In an Italian criticism, Marcello Pagnini says that "Conrad Aiken has within him the rhythmical sense of the universe."[14] Whatever this statement may mean, it is surely true that the "rhythmical sense" in this case is scarcely suitable to the poem's conception. The poem is far from communicating the values of its subject.

III

The best of Aiken's most recent poetry has been collected in three volumes; some of the poems in them are among the finest in the American language. They have the characteristic rhythmical gift, but they are more than just rhymed maneuvers through thematic jungles. *Skylight One,* the first of these publications,[15] contains fifteen shorter poems, some of them memorable and true. "Mayflower" (5-9) has much more the sense of Aiken's subject than the whole of *The Kid.* The "ancient voices" speak to the poet "in the New England spring." And the echoes of Puritan New England are authentic. It is an obituary of the New England spirit, saying many of the things his long essay of 1937 had said. The names of flower and plant echo from the past,

> Yet even so, though in the observance kept,
> here most of all where first our fathers stept,
> was something of the spirit that became idle, and at last
> lost all that love; and heard no more
> the voices singing from a distant shore.
>
> (*Skylight,* 6)

The dream of the West is also communicated, as it was more spectacularly and less surely in *Landscape West of Eden.* The bodies in "God's Acre" all face to the west: "What dream was this of a more perfect rest."

> Or were they sceptics, and perforce, in doubt,
> wistful to watch the last of the light go out?
> (*Skylight*, 7)

Something of that haunted sense of the past, of Frost's "Directive," is beautifully communicated. As in the Frost poem, ruins bespeak ghosts, the return of life and animation to inert matter:

> And the blue lilacs, the grey laylocks, take possession
> round every haunted cellar-hole, like an obsession:
> keep watch in the dead houses, on vanished stairs;
> (*Skylight*, 8)

"Crepe Myrtle" is a threnody on the occasion of the death of Franklin Delano Roosevelt in 1945. The cemetery wall is testimony of death; a handful of leaves "dances on the moonlit wall of an old house, opens / silent fingers, closes them again . . ." (*Skylight*, 11). The rhythms define the slow progress of the body to its burial:

> The coffin of the great man travels slowly
> slowly and well through the seasons, the spring passing
> over into the rich summer, and with the earth
> revolves under the changing arch of the years.
> (*Skylight*, 13)

The reflections of the Preludes are also to be found in these poems but dispersed; there are no magnificent close patterns of thought, but exercises in it, within frames especially chosen for it. "Voyage to Spring" presents the "trap" of nature, the quick bright colors that are so quickly gone, the "chromatic deception, / the viridescent treason . . ." (*Skylight*, 17).

> . . . The mirage of spring
> shatters about us in a broken prison of rainbows
> never to be assembled again, or to be assembled
> only in the ironic despair of a dream:
> (*Skylight*, 19)

There is a sense of deception in all of the ceremonies, natural and human, which fill our lives. We use them to hide from us the tragedies and brutalities that underlie the surface, never trying to see them as they are, hoping that they will not be shown too near us. We are, therefore, given to improvisations in order to gain time or to seclude ourselves: "And the rituals, the formalities, the prepared language, / how inadequate to the occasion: for none exist" (*Skylight*, 23).

The idea of ceremony as a disguise, a lifelong improvisation of our thoughts and gestures, is an attractive one. Rarely do the reflections in nature of human emotional values receive so eloquent or effective an expression as in this poem: "always the giant step from island to island of being," the poet says, of the seasons, of lives changing and giving way, "terrified yet fearless over the infinite, / precisely as the celandine steps from November / to blind April . . ." (*Skylight*, 25). "The Improvisation" may be thought Conrad Aiken's special kind of poetic form; it is the envelope into which his thought most surely slips.

Much the same can be said of "The Clover," though the conceit is slighter and the expression too much in the manner of his earlier, unsuccessful calls to the infinite.

> Pray, time, what is our shame
> or what this blessedness without a name
> that the unknown of love should come to this
> animal birth embodied in a kiss?
>
> (*Skylight*, 29)

The pattern of life and death and of their being imaged in dreams is skillfully given: as time "is turned as sand by the hand is turned," so night succeeds day, and waking is an uncertain renewal of the day (*Skylight*, 30).

"Hallowe'en" is an elaborate ceremonial play on the facts of death and the dead; the superstitions impressed upon the ceremony all point to the *memento mori*.

> at Samhain, the end of summer,
> salt smell of kelp mixed with scent of the windfall
> and whirled up the chalk path at daybreak,
> we sacrificed a white horse to the sun-god
> and kindled great fires on the hills
>
> (*Skylight*, 35)

The poem eventually turns to the figure of Aiken's grandfather, William James Potter, whom he celebrates in a forenote to the volume, and to whom Aiken seems much indebted for his "New

England" and his American sense. You "at the dark's edge," he says, "revenant again to complain and to haunt me,"

> cavorting at the fire's edge, leaping through the flames,
> while the moon, behind Sheepfold Hill,
> lights her old bonfire . . .
>
> (*Skylight,* 37)

"Everlasting," the poem which apparently should have given the book its clue, is not successful; it is once again a substitution of performance for thought. The *Skylight One* of the poem, from which it takes its title, is the bombing place of the atomic experiment;[16] and apparently this poem is designed to treat of the historical release of the atom bomb. But the melodramatics of the occasion elude the poet's sight.

> Sadeyes under Skylight One, waiting for the vision
> to be fractured, refracted, atomized,
> the giver and the receiver,
> the recorder and the achiever,
> two lovers awaiting the moment
> when the unimaginable lightning will come over
>
> (*Skylight,* 42)

Generally the volume fully justifies itself in the sense in which Julian Symons describes it, as "in some ways an excellent introduction to Aiken's work, for it is a collection that shows very well the various sides of his talent."[17] The attractiveness of the volume is that it shows Aiken working surely and confidently within the terms set up and explained in the Preludes.

A Letter from Li Po and Other Poems[18] is similarly ingratiating. The long title poem is a tribute to the great Chinese poet, some of whose poems Ezra Pound so effectively adapted in *Cathay* (1915). There are echoes of Li Po here, but Aiken does not allow the Chinese poet to interfere with his customary, quite un-Oriental conceptions and rhythms. Whatever may be said in the way of putting him in line with ancient Chinese thought, the evidence is strikingly modern, drawing directly from the Preludes. The "alchemy by which we grow" is

> . . . the self becoming word, the word
> becoming world. And with each part we play
> we add to cosmic *Sum* and cosmic sum.

> Who knows but one day we shall find,
> hidden in the prism at the rainbow's foot,
> the square root of the eccentric absolute,
> and the concentric absolute to come.
>
> (*Li Po,* 18)

These quoted lines sum up the position neatly: the intimate relation of the self to word, the act of speech being the act of self-identification; the move beyond self to world-definition; and finally, the "eccentric absolute" and the "concentric absolute," which exactly phrase the process of interrelationship between self and cosmos that Aiken has been presenting almost throughout his career. There is the same play of thing against word in the lines that follow: ". . . The living word / springs from the dying, as leaves in spring / spring from dead leaves, our birth from death" (*Li Po,* 22). *Li Po* is a review of the ideas in *Preludes for Memnon* and especially of those in *Time in the Rock.* The created poem is emphasized in *Li Po* as the ultimate "absolute" creation, in which evil "like a brushstroke" will disappear, "in the last perfect rhyme / of the begin-all-end-all poem, time" (28).

"The Logos in Fifth Avenue" is a form of *Brownstone Eclogues* summary of the city: the city and its people alternating with somber question-answer prose, and unattractive witticisms. In the end the thought is characteristically an acceptance note. The observer does not in Aiken's poems go beyond this point of acceptance; or, if he does, he does so in peril. But acceptance is not self-negation; it is an end-result of a creative compromise with chaos. The "pattern" is a product of the self's going forward to define the experience of being.

> Stay, stay
> the hand upon the bough upon the heart
> stand still o love o living art
> that in the blood and in the sap and in the sun
> as in our mythic dream last night
> bids all remain unchanged:
> urge now your love for all things demiurge
> for that is he and that is we
> and bid this pattern be.
>
> (*Li Po,* 42)

The same may be said for "Overture to Today." The poet is in
a state of creative ecstasy; his conception of the divine is the
divine itself.

> we who divine
> divine ourselves, divine our own divinity
> it is the examination
> of godhead by godhead
> the imagination
> of that which it is to be divine.
>
> (*Li Po,* 77)

The emphasis upon human creativity in these lines makes a
perfect Aiken–Stevens sense. The creative mode is the imagination, the "world becoming word" (80). Aiken puts more and
more stress upon the fact of creation, less and less upon its
insuperable difficulty. It is as though the universe had finally
been "tamed," our own sense of its turbulence diminished. There
is more emphasis upon the scene, the specific ground upon which
the act of creation is performed. But we are each of us, as we
always were before, caught in an act of imitative, creative
magic: tying our tie, walking along the shore or in the sun,
making peach trees bloom and grow. We superintend the
process of things-becoming-pattern-becoming-word-becoming-art,
perhaps as the poet Li Po encouraged Aiken to believe.

The pattern is continued, though not so successfully, in *Sheepfold Hill:*[19] the appeal to seek peace for ourselves in a balance
of natural and human act.

> Come, let us seek in ourselves, while time includes us,
> the illusions whorled and whirling center;
> and praise the imperishable metal of that flower
> whose seed was barren grain.
>
> ("Maya"; *Hill,* 39)

Perhaps the most interesting poem in this recent collection[20]
is "Herman Melville," a tribute to an American hero to whom
Aiken has already addressed much trust. For he thinks of Melville's having turned the American mind away from its transcendental, easy liberalism to knowledge and a sense of evil. Melville
is still within the early range of American intellectual history:
individualistic, the idea of the self's being closely associated with
the creative process still strong within him.

Between him and Aiken, Henry and Brooks Adams intervened; for the entire range of Aiken's thought is not transcendental, but naturalistic. Perhaps this poem, as well as others in the last three volumes, suggests a moderate and modified return to the days of his Unitarian grandfather, William Potter. At any rate, the formula of "world becoming word" is a form of readjustment, the naturalistic world (which frightened so many of Aiken's characters) coming 'round to the self–world relationship suggested in early nineteenth-century thought. Melville is admired, however, not for having compromised the problem of self, but for the *fiat* declaration of man's tragic stature:

> and straight he knew as known before
> the Logos in Leviathan's roar
> he deepest sounding with his lead
> who all had fathomed all had said.
>
> (*Hill*, 46)

IV

The great difficulty in assessing Conrad Aiken's value is the tremendous range and variety of his work. Most modern American writers were, whether careful or fortunate in it, successful in pointing their reputations to a fairly limited focus of achieved excellence; or they have, like Faulkner, stayed within the range of one genre. Aiken's forty-two titles include twenty-nine of poetry, four collections of short stories, four novels, two collections of criticism, one play, and one autobiographical "essay." The major work is, of course, the poetry. But even in this form the range of good and bad is so great and the outpouring so richly diffuse that it requires a demonstrable patience to come to a mature judgment of the whole of it.

The general reaction to him is well represented in this statement by George Dillon: the bad pages "grossly outnumber the good ones"; the mass of it is made of "skillful patchworks of loquacious, lazily turned phraseology."[21] R. P. Blackmur, one of a few "patient readers" of Aiken, suggests that his poetry is "all alike, and has often been complained of, on that account, by dull readers."[22] The impatience is pardonable.

Aiken presents an imaginative gift extremely rare in modern literature, in any literature. But he has not been timid, or cautious, in the exercising of it. Worse, he has often squandered the talent and published the results too quickly and easily. Nevertheless, he is one of our underrated, "neglected" figures.[23] He has not "caught on." Always there, with rarely a year without a publication of one kind or another, he has nevertheless been passed over for reputations made by writers who "struck it rich" in a favorable time and who have successfully extended them since.[24]

The question of "major" and "minor" is perhaps irrelevant. In a sense, there are only major poems, not major poets. This fact has often been ignored in the "personality cultism" that has plagued modern literary reputations. Aiken seems also to have arrived "too late" to make an independent consideration of his work possible. And the cumulative result is that he has been tagged an imitator, a subservient "me-too-er." Nothing could be further from the truth. Despite evidences and echoes—usually in poems Aiken chose not to reprint—his is a distinctive manner and an extraordinarily skillful genius.

Perhaps his greatest contribution has been in a type of "coming to terms" literature. Very sensitive to the meanings of modern naturalism—a fact that is undoubtedly traceable in part to the tragedy of his childhood—Aiken first tried to meet this defeating knowledge in elaborate romantic retreats from it and then with an excessive virtuosity in romantic declamations of a "*j'existe, et rien n'importe*" pose. But even in the worst of these, there is a sense of a growing maturity of the role of language and art in the matter of adjusting to and understanding the modern situation.

I should say the most remarkable fact of his career is his having moved from a romantic to a "metaphysical" mode of intellectual analysis and representation. The "Symphonies" are too often falsely "musical," self-consciously maneuvered in the interests of a theory; the poetic values which result are inappropriate to what the poems are trying to say, or they get in the way of saying it. As he turns to the Preludes, Aiken shows again and again—often in the least ambitious of his poems—a competence in fitting the word to the thought, with results sometimes resembling Stevens at his best, sometimes quite distinctively his own.

The real issue of Aiken's poetry is a "metaphysical" problem, and it needs to be solved metaphysically. That is, there are many of the intellectual and emotional difficulties and paradoxes that haunt seventeenth-century metaphysical poetry; but the essential paradox (as well as the means of its resolution) does not and cannot exist for Aiken. The paradoxes of time and eternity were real and viable for Donne and his contemporaries—as indeed they are for Eliot; but they cannot be indulged in, or meaningfully employed, in Aiken's poetry. This is a major reason for his having resorted for so long to what, for want of a better name, must be called "romantic naturalism."

The Preludes of *Preludes for Memnon* and *Time in the Rock* offer a new composite intellectual image in modern poetry. I have discussed it several times, but should like very briefly to restate it in this final summary. It is the self peering *through*—not *at*, though in the illusion of staring *at*—a glass into the universe, in which he sees himself as a part of the chaos he is observing. It is an inversion of the transcendentalist vision, in which the self projects creatively, performing god-like acts of concentric maneuvering. Always in Aiken, the image returns to the observer, and the challenge to him—far greater than any offered the nineteenth-century American, or at least understood by him—is to *accept* the paradoxical isolation that is his lot.

The poetry will, therefore, be a constant forward–retreat–encircling motion, the language and the lines moving ahead hesitantly toward statement, never quite satisfactorily achieving it. It is, as Blackmur has said of it, the drama of the "enacting consciousness," and the poetry is the act itself. This can permit neither easy resolutions nor melodramatic cries of despair (there is no one about to hear them in any case).

What the Preludes do in the poetry, the situational drama does in the fiction. As "Mr. Arcularis" and other stories will testify, the problems and paradoxes are also present in the fiction. But the most important fictional strategy is the psychoanalytic. *Great Circle* is the most remarkable use of it.

Here as well, the hero must come to terms with himself; the self is shattered by a childhood experience, the equivalent of the death so frequently used as a coordinate in the Preludes. One must come "the long way back," must see himself within the scene of which he is the observer; this is true of Andy Cather and it is abundantly true of the observer in the Preludes. Aiken's value is great indeed, though he has been slow in giving it to us; we may almost say "reluctant to give it away."

Notes and References

Chapter One

1. *Ushant* (New York, 1952), p. 302. Italics mine.
2. See Houston Peterson, *The Melody of Chaos* (New York, 1931), p. 27. Hereafter referred to in text as *Melody*.
3. *Obsessive Images*, ed. by W. V. O'Connor (Minneapolis, 1960), p. 62.
4. Quoted in *Freudianism and the Literary Mind*, 2nd ed. (Baton Rouge, La., 1957), p. 281.
5. Review of *Collected Poems*, New York *Post*, July 20, 1929. Reprinted in *A Reviewer's ABC*, ed. by Rufus A. Blanshard (New York, 1958), p. 267. Hereafter referred to in text as *ABC*.
6. Quoted by George Boas in *The Philosophy of George Santayana*, ed. by Paul A. Schilpp (New York, 1940), p. 245.
7. *Among the Lost People* (New York, 1934), pp. 238-39. Hereafter referred to in text as *Lost People*.
8. *The Expense of Greatness* (New York, 1940), p. 222. Originally in the *Southern Review* (Winter, 1937).
9. Only five of the *Scepticisms* pieces are reprinted in *ABC*.
10. *Wake*, XI, (1952), 56.
11. *Scepticisms* (New York, 1919), p. 61.
12. Aiken was, in fact, an early sponsor of Emily Dickinson's verse; in 1924 he edited a selection of it for English readers (London, 1924). The quotation above can also be found in Aiken's introduction to that volume.
13. He calls Alfred Kreymborg's poetry (of *Mushrooms*) the "poetic paraphrase of the lisp and coo . . ." (*Scepticisms*, 247).
14. "Poet of Creative Dissolution," *Wake*, XI, (1952), 102.
15. See below, Chapters 3-6, for a full discussion of Aiken's poetry.
16. *Conversation* (New York, 1940), p. 160.

Chapter Two

1. *Wake*, XI (1952), 81.
2. A study of the omissions from *The Short Stories of Conrad Aiken* (New York, 1950) demonstrates once again Aiken's shrewdness and honesty as a critic of his own work. Without exception, the stories he chose not to reprint are his worst. Omitted from *Bring! Bring!*: "The Escape from Fatuity," "The Orange Moth," "The Letter,"

Notes and References

"Soliloquy on a Park Bench." Omitted from *Among the Lost People:* "O How She Laughed!", "No, No, Go Not to Lethe," "Pure as the Driven Snow." Omitted from *Costumes by Eros:* "The Necktie," "The Professor's Escape," "All, All Wasted," "A Conversation," "The Woman Hater," "West End," "The Moment."

3. *Skylight One* (New York, 1949), n.p.

4. He bears the family name as the second of his: Conrad *Potter* Aiken.

5. *Poetry*, LXXVI (June, 1950), 165.

6. "The Poetry of Conrad Aiken," *Wake*, XI (1952), 108.

7. Not in any of the three volumes, this story first appeared in *The Short Stories of Conrad Aiken*, pp. 327-39.

8. See Mark Schorer's analysis, "The Life in the Fiction," *Wake*, XI (1952), 57-60.

9. "Strange Moonlight," in *Bring! Bring! and Other Stories* (New York, 1952), p. 44.

10. In *Among the Lost People*, pp. 128-57.

11. Discussed above. See Chapter I, pp. 21-22.

12. *Among the Lost People*, pp. 12-43.

13. *Mr. Arcularis* (Cambridge, Mass., 1957).

14. *Great Circle* (New York, 1933), p. 8.

15. *Bring! Bring! and Other Stories*, pp. 171-85.

16. *Ibid.*, pp. 93-103.

17. (London, 1939). Hereafter referred to in text as *Heart*.

18. See *The Bridge*, in *Collected Poems* (New York, 1933), pp. 13-18.

19. *Bring! Bring! and Other Stories*, pp. 186-210.

20. *Ibid.*, pp. 120-31.

21. *Ibid.*, pp. 104-19.

22. (New York, 1935). Hereafter referred to in text as *Coffin*.

23. (New York, 1928). Hereafter referred to in text as *Eros*.

24. *Among the Lost People*, pp. 246-92.

25. *Costumes by Eros*, pp. 183-98.

26. *Ibid.*, pp. 213-28.

27. *Ibid.*, pp. 49-60.

28. *Ibid.*, pp. 86-116.

29. *Ibid.*, pp. 3-28.

30. *Ibid.*, pp. 61-83.

31. *Ibid.*, pp. 139-48.

32. *Ibid.*, pp. 151-79.

33. (New York, 1940).

34. *Costumes by Eros*, pp. 29-56.

35. (New York, 1927). Hereafter referred to in text as *Voyage*.

36. This scene is not unlike those in the "Circe" episode of Joyce's

Ulysses, and it has a source very similar to it: the unconscious of the "young man": Dedalus or Demarest.

37. See above, Chapter I, pp. 25-27.

38. See F. J. Hoffman, *Freudianism and the Literary Mind,* second edition, pp. 278-79; Melvin Friedman, *Stream of Consciousness* (New Haven, 1955), pp. 247-49.

Chapter Three

1. *New Poets from Old* (Columbia University Press, 1940), pp. 291-306.

2. "The Poetry of Conrad Aiken," *Wake,* XI (1952), 113.

3. *The Expense of Greatness,* pp. 218-19.

4. "Pilgrim's Progress: Conrad Aiken's Poetry," *Texas Quarterly,* I (Winter, 1958), 138.

5. See Aiken's 1919 essay (originally in *Scepticisms*), "Magic or Legerdemain?" (*ABC,* 41-45), in which he speaks of a "subconscious treasure."

6. "The Author of John Deth," *New Republic,* LXVIII (July 22, 1931), 266.

7. *More Modern American Poets* (New York, 1954), p. 67. The poem Southworth has specifically in mind is *The House of Dust.*

8. *The Harvard Advocate Anthology* (New York, 1950), pp. 119-26.

9. *Harvard Advocate,* issue of February, 1910.

10. *Ibid.,* issue of June, 1910.

11. *Ibid.,* issue of February, 1911.

12. (New York, 1914).

13. This is the poem Blanshard has called *The Clerk's Journal,* "Pilgrim's Progress," *op. cit.,* p. 136.

14. (Boston, 1916). Edition used: *Collected Poems* (New York, 1953), pp. 3-25. Hereafter referred to in text as *CP.*

15. (Boston, 1917).

16. *Appearance and Reality* (Oxford, 1893; ninth impression, 1930). Quoted by Eliot in *Complete Poems and Plays* (New York, 1952), p. 54.

Chapter Four

1. "The Poetry of Conrad Aiken," *Nation,* CXXXIII (October 14, 1931), 393-94.

2. *The Collected Poems of Wallace Stevens* (New York, 1955), p. 240.

3. Kunitz, *op. cit.,* p. 394.

4. First published in *Poetry,* XIV (June, 1919), 152-59. Edition used, in *ABC,* pp. 126-30.

5. See above, Chapter I, pp. 27-29.

6. In *On Poets and Poetry* (New York, 1957), p. 32.

7. *The New Criticism* (Norfolk, Conn., 1941), pp. 294-336.

8. (Athens, Georgia).

9. Written in 1915; published in Boston, Four Seas, 1918, with *Senlin.* Edition used: *CP,* 26-54. A few words are in order concerning Aiken's habits of revision. Of *Charnel Rose* he said that it presented "an almost insoluble problem in surgery" (*CP,* 863), and that in its first edition it was "half again as long" as it was in *The Divine Pilgrim* (*CP,* 864). A line count shows that the difference is between 1,146 lines, in the first edition, and 882 lines; this means that the first publication is about one-third longer.

More interesting than this statistical matter are the kinds of changes Aiken made. They are almost invariably designed to make the poem more precise, to eliminate vague words, phrases, lines, passages, and to sharpen the focus of meaning. Since the meaning is in any case imprecise, the changes are only minimally helpful. They do bring the idea of the poem more easily to the reader's attention, but the "surgery" of which Aiken speaks contributes little enough to the health of the patient. Examples of what he omitted will help to make one appreciate his concern:

> Irises gleaming, and roses conceived anew,
> And the pale little leaves that gave her tender mirth,
> And fledgling birds that now for the first time flew;
> (p. 96 of 1918 edition)

> Music that cried intense, but after
> Shuddered down to livid laughter.
> (p. 103)

> Cold ripples chuckle, white bubbles whisper,
> Your face is drowsy with love.
> You stretch slow arms in the moonlight
> And pretend to be watching the skies.
> (p. 122)

Revisions of lines that Aiken retained are interesting for what they show of Aiken's striving for economy of language:

> He looked with loathing in her eyes:
> Hideous void of twilight skies;
> Evening skies with bats therein.

He saw thick powder upon her skin.
This was not she! . . .
> (1918 ed., p. 106)

becomes:

Whose were these loathed and empty eyes?
Who, falling, in these wingless skies?
This was not she . . .
> (*CP*, 30)

The revision of the following lines consists primarily of cutting out excessive fat from the tissue:

Saw gorgeous roses fall apart,
Each to disclose a charnel heart,
Each of them with a toad at heart.
> (1918 ed., p. 104)

becomes:

He watched red roses drop apart
Each to disclose a charnel heart.
> (*CP*, 29)

In addition there are many changes and excisions of word and phrase: *flash* for *shine; crowding* for *many; batlike* for *swiftly; thought* for *mused,* several times; *pure text of dust* for *sweet mouths of dust; swarmed* for *whirled; texture* for *flame; motionless eye* for *sinister eye* (the word *sinister* being several times cut); etc.

10. Kunitz, *op. cit.,* p. 393.

11. Written, 1915-1916; published in Boston by Four Seas, 1916. Edition used: *CP,* 54-114.

12. See "The Comedian as the Letter C" (1923), in *The Collected Poems,* pp. 27-46.

13. *Bring! Bring! and Other Stories,* pp. 56-92.

14. Written in 1916-1917; published in Boston by Four Seas, 1920.

15. "Preludes: IV," *Complete Poems and Plays,* p. 13.

16. *New Poets from Old,* p. 297.

17. *Complete Poems,* pp. 93-99.

18. Published with the *Charnel Rose* (Boston, 1918). First written, 1918. Edition used: *CP,* pp. 195-222. *Senlin* underwent two major revisions, according to Aiken: the first, "considerably revised for the Hogarth Press edition in 1925"; the second (in *The Divine Pilgrim* and in *CP*) "in some instances back to the original" (*CP,* 864). The second revision leaves the poem much as it was in its first

edition. Changes, however, are sometimes interesting as signs of Aiken's concern for the right word and phrase. For example, "I am a desolate room" becomes "I am a room of rock"; "a white sand shore" becomes "a coral shore"; "tired grass" becomes "withered grass"; "On flourishing arms" becomes "on flailing arms." Omissions (many fewer than in the case of *Charnel Rose*) are designed to cut out irrelevancies and vague "color": "Drunk with excess" is omitted from "The long red sun-rays glancing"; "What is it that wars in the sunlight on this hill?" becomes "what war in sunlight on this hill?" Some thirty-six lines are omitted from the first edition, for the same reasons that motivated the much more drastic omissions from *Charnel Rose*. In general, one may say that the revisions of *Senlin* do it more good than those of *Charnel Rose* helped it; this is a simple enough inference from the fact of the initial superiority of *Senlin* to its companion poem.

19. "The Floodlit Mind," *Wake*, XI (1952), 37.
20. Written, 1919-1920; published in New York by Knopf, 1923. Edition used: *CP*, 222-76.
21. Wallace Stevens, *Collected Poems*, p. 28.
22. Hamilton, *op. cit.*, p. 45.
23. First written, 1925. Edition used: *CP*, 276-88, where it is "reprinted as written."
24. In *Collected Poems*, pp. 66-70.
25. Symons, *op. cit.*, p. 113.

Chapter Five

1. (New York, 1921).
2. (Cambridge, Mass., 1922). Edition used: CP, 383-96.
3. *John Deth, A Metaphysical Legend, and Other Poems* (New York, 1930). Edition used: *CP*, 397-443. The title poem was first published in *The Second American Caravan* (1928), an anthology of new writing.
4. In the 1925 revision of *Priapus and the Pool* (New York).
5. In *Turns and Movies*, 1916.
6. "If a Man Die," *Wake*, XI (1952), 50-56.
7. (New York, 1931). Edition used: *CP*, 498-573.
8. Originally published by Harvard University Press in 1910. Edition used is one of Anchor Books (1953), p. 16.
9. See Aiken's "Gigantic Dreams," *New Republic*, LV (June 27, 1928), 146-47.
10. Cf. Wallace Stevens, "The Idea of Order at Key West" (*Collected Poems*, pp. 128-30):

She was the single artificer of the world
In which she sang. And when she sang, the sea,
Whatever self it had, became the self
That was her song, for she was the maker . . .

(p. 129)

11. "Mr. Aiken's Second Wind," *New Republic*, LXXXIX (January 13, 1937), 335.

12. *Complete Poems and Plays*, p. 118.

13. (New York, 1936). Hereafter referred to in text as *Rock*.

14. *Southern Review*, II (Winter, 1937), 558-76.

15. In *Collected Poems*, pp. 380-408. Originally published in Cummington, Mass., in 1942.

Chapter Six

1. This does not include publications (by small presses) of poems that appear in other volumes. Nor does it include *The Divine Pilgrim* (University of Georgia Press, 1949), a rearrangement and sometimes a revision of the "Symphonies." See Bibliography below, pp. 164-65, for a complete list of Aiken's titles in the order of their publication.

2. (New York, 1931). Hereafter referred to in text as *Osiris Jones*.

3. (New York, 1935). Hereafter referred to in text as *Eden*.

4. See Marianne Moore's full discussion of this poem in "If a Man Die," pp. 50-53.

5. See my essay, "Freedom and Conscious Form," *Virginia Quarterly Review*, XXXVII (Spring, 1961), 269-85.

6. (New York, 1940). Edition used: *CP*, 758-78, which appears to differ from the first edition only in occasional capitalizations, where the original used lower case.

7. (New York, 1942). Hereafter referred to in text as *Eclogues*.

8. See Donald Stauffer in *Poets at Work* (New York, 1948), pp. 72-76.

9. See *Collected Poems*, pp. 40-41.

10. Other poems in the volume include a long and rather successful tribute to García Lorca ("The Poet in Granada," pp. 85-95).

11. (Norfolk, Conn., 1944).

12. (New York, 1947).

13. See *ABC*, pp. 82-93.

14. "The Myth of William Blackstone," trans. by Janet B. Morgan, *Wake*, XI (1952), 70.

15. (New York, 1949). Hereafter referred to in text as *Skylight*.

16. See Arvid Shulenberger, *Poetry*, LXXVI (June, 1950), 166.

17. "The Poetry of Conrad Aiken," *Wake*, XI (1952), 112.

18. (New York, 1955). Hereafter referred to in text as *Li Po*.

19. (New York, 1958). Hereafter referred to in text as *Hill*.

20. *Sheepfold Hill* includes three poems already published in *Skylight One*: "Hallowe'en," "Mayflower," and "Crepe Myrtle."

21. "Mr. Aiken's Poetry," *Poetry*, XXXVII (January, 1931), 225. Robert W. Stallman provides an interesting summary of the critical reactions in "Checklist on Conrad Aiken," *Wake*, XI (1952), 114-21.

22. *New Republic*, LXI (January 22, 1930), 255.

23. I use the term "neglected" in the expectation that it will shortly prove ill-advised. Studies of Aiken are being prepared; perhaps the best of them will be Rufus Blanshard's, if his essays so far published are a reliable clue.

24. The results of this mistaken estimate are no more evident than in Edward Dahlberg's ridiculous review of *Ushant*, in *Poetry*, LXXXI (February, 1953), 313-21.

Selected Bibliography

WORKS BY AIKEN

(Arranged in order of publication.)

Earth Triumphant and Other Tales in Verse. New York: Macmillan, 1914.

Turns and Movies and Other Tales in Verse. Boston: Houghton, Mifflin, 1961.

The Jig of Forslin: A Symphony. Boston: Four Seas, 1916.

Nocturne of Remembered Spring and Other Poems. Boston: Four Seas, 1917.

The Charnel Rose; Senlin: A Biography, and Other Poems. Boston: Four Seas, 1918.

Scepticisms: Notes on Contemporary Poetry. New York: Knopf, 1919.

The House of Dust: A Symphony. Boston: Four Seas, 1920.

Punch: The Immortal Liar. New York: Knopf, 1921.

Priapus and the Pool. Cambridge, Mass.: Dunster House, 1922.

The Pilgrimage of Festus. New York, Knopf, 1923.

Priapus and the Pool and Other Poems. New York: Boni and Liveright, 1925.

Bring! Bring! and Other Stories. New York: Boni and Liveright, 1925.

Blue Voyage, a Novel. New York: Scribner's, 1927.

Costumes by Eros, Stories. New York: Scribner's, 1928.

Prelude. New York: Random House, 1929.

Selected Poems. New York: Scribner's, 1929.

John Deth, A Metaphysical Legend, and Other Poems. New York: Scribner's, 1930.

The Coming Forth by Day of Osiris Jones. New York: Scribner's, 1931.

Preludes for Memnon. New York: Scribner's, 1931.

Prelude: A Poem. New York: Equinox, 1932.

And in the Hanging Gardens. Baltimore: Garamond, 1933.

Great Circle, a Novel. New York: Scribner's, 1933.

Selected Bibliography

Among the Lost People, Short Stories. New York, Scribner's, 1934.

Landscape West of Eden. New York: Scribner's, 1935.

King Coffin, a Novel. New York: Scribner's, 1935.

Time in the Rock: Preludes to Definition. New York: Scribner's, 1936.

A Heart for the Gods of Mexico, a Novel. London: Martin Secker, 1939.

And in the Human Heart. New York: Duell, Sloan, and Pearce, 1940.

Conversation: Or, Pilgrim's Progress, a Novel. New York: Duell, Sloan, and Pearce, 1940.

Brownstone Eclogues and Other Poems. New York: Duell, Sloan, and Pearce, 1942.

The Soldier: A Poem. Norfolk, Conn.: New Directions, 1944.

The Kid. New York: Duell, Sloan, and Pearce, 1947.

Skylight One: Fifteen Poems. New York: Oxford University Press, 1949.

The Divine Pilgrim. Athens: University of Georgia Press, 1949.

The Short Stories of Conrad Aiken. New York: Duell, Sloan, and Pearce, 1950.

Ushant: An Essay. New York and Boston: Duell, Sloan, and Pearce, and Little, Brown, 1952.

Collected Poems. New York: Oxford University Press, 1953.

A Letter from Li Po and Other Poems. New York: Oxford University Press, 1955.

Mr. Arcularis, a Play. Cambridge, Mass.: Harvard University Press, 1957.

Sheepfold Hill: Fifteen Poems. New York: Sagamore Press, 1958.

A Reviewer's ABC. Ed. Rufus A. Blanshard. New York: Meridian Press, 1958.

Selected Poems. New York: Oxford University Press, 1961.

STUDIES OF CONRAD AIKEN

I *Checklists*

Note: The following checklists, though partial, are useful supplementary listings of Aiken's writings and of studies of him:

Blanshard, Rufus A. "Checklist of Conrad Aiken's Critical Writings," in *A Reviewer's ABC* (New York, 1958), pp. 395-408.

Stallman, R. W. "Annotated Checklist on Conrad Aiken: A Critical Study," *Wake*, XI, (1952), 114-21.

II   *A Selected List of Essays and Parts of Books on Aiken*

NOTE: The only book-length study of Aiken to date is Houston Peterson's *The Melody of Chaos* (New York, 1931), long since out of print. There is biographical matter in it, and the author quotes from letters received from Aiken. But the book is primarily a study of Aiken's work to 1930 and of its relationships to *milieu*. As I have pointed out in my text, Peterson's book was published before Aiken's major poetry was available. Other new books on Aiken are likely to appear soon. In my preparation of this study, I have used only materials available in periodicals and books; I have not consulted the manuscripts of any other books on Aiken.

BEACH, JOSEPH WARREN. *Obsessive Images: Symbolism in Poetry of the 1930's and 1940's* (Minneapolis: Univ. of Minnesota Press, 1960), pp. 62-69. Some remarks on the "imagery of terror," under the general heading, "The Secret Terror in the Heart."

BLACKMUR, RICHARD P. "The Day before the Daybreak," *Poetry*, XL (April, 1932), 39-44.

————. Review of *Selected Poems*, *New Republic*, XLI (January 22, 1930), 255-56.

————. "Mr. Aiken's Second Wind," *New Republic*, LXXXIX (January 13, 1937), 335.

————. "The Composition in Nine Poets," *Southern Review*, II (Winter, 1937), 558-76. Reprinted in *The Expense of Greatness* (New York: Arrow Editions, 1940), pp. 199-223. Since Blackmur was the most intelligent of contemporary reviewers of Aiken's poetry, all of these items are valuable, but the last of them is especially acute and useful.

BLANSHARD, RUFUS A. "Pilgrim's Progress: Conrad Aiken's Poetry," *Texas Quarterly*, I (Winter, 1958), 135-48. The best single essay on Aiken, this is both an analysis of certain poems and a plea for Aiken as a major poet.

————. "Metamorphosis of a Dream," *Sewanee Review*, LXV (Autumn, 1957), 694-702. On *Mr. Arcularis, A Play*.

BROWN, CALVIN S. "Something Old, Something New," *Wake*, XI (1952), 90-94. On *Skylight One*.

COWLEY, MALCOLM. "Biography With Letters," *Wake*, XI (1952), 26-31. A tribute, with some reminiscences.

DAHLBERG, EDWARD. "A Long Lotus Sleep," *Poetry*, LXXXI (February, 1953), 313-21. A diatribe on *Ushant*, which accuses Aiken of lacking vigor and wasting his time in experiment.

Selected Bibliography

DILLON, GEORGE. "Mr. Aiken's Poetry," *Poetry*, XXXVII (January, 1931), 221-25. Unfavorable, but suggests that Aiken has "promise."

EDISON, GEORGE. "Thematic Symbols in the Poetry of Aiken and MacLeish," *University of Toronto Quarterly*, X (October, 1940), 12-26. A look at certain dominating themes.

FRIEDMAN, MELVIN. *Stream of Consciousness: A Study in Literary Method* (New Haven: Yale Univ. Press, 1955), pp. 247-50. Some notes, chiefly on *Blue Voyage*.

GARRIGUE, JEAN. "A Consideration of Mr. Arcularis, the Play," *Wake*, XI (1952), 73-79. Impressions of author's reaction to the play.

GREGORY, HORACE, and ZATURENSKA, MARYA. *A History of American Poetry: 1900-1940* (New York: Harcourt, Brace, 1946), pp. 217-25. Credits Aiken with some isolated excellence, but generally unfavorable.

HAMILTON, G. ROSTREVOR. "The Floodlit Mind," *Wake*, XI (1952), 32-48. An intelligent study of *Senlin, Punch* and *Festus*.

HOFFMAN, FREDERICK J. *Freudianism and the Literary Mind* (Baton Rouge, La.: Louisiana State Univ. Press, 1957), pp. 274-81. Also in Evergreen Books (New York, 1959). Concerns Aiken's relationship to psychoanalysis and his use of stream-of-consciousness techniques, principally in the fiction.

KUNITZ, STANLEY. "The Poetry of Conrad Aiken," *Nation*, CXXXIII (October 14, 1931), 393-94. An intelligent, balanced review.

LOWRY, MALCOLM. "A Letter," *Wake*, XI (1952), 80-89. A personal tribute.

MOORE, MARIANNE. "If a Man Die," *Hound and Horn*, V (1932), 313-20; reprinted, with slight revision, in *Wake*, XI (1952), 50-56. An excellent study of *Osiris Jones* and *Preludes for Memnon*.

MURRAY, HENRY A. "Poet of Creative Dissolution," *Wake*, XI (1952), 95-106. Personal tribute of a psychiatrist friend.

PAGNINI, MARCELLO. "The Myth of William Blackstone." Trans. by Janet B. Morgan. *Wake*, XI (1952), 61-72. On *The Kid*. A rather elaborate explanation of Aiken's poem of American history and folklore, *The Kid*, this essay suffers from a failure to appreciate the American idiom and praises extravagantly a mediocre poem.

REIN, DAVID M. "Conrad Aiken and Psychoanalysis," *Psychoanalytic Review*, XLII (October, 1955), 402-11.

SCHORER, MARK. "The Life in the Fiction," *Wake,* XI (1952), 57-60. On "Life Is Not a Short Story."

SCHWARTZ, DELMORE. "Merry-Go-Round of Opinion," *New Republic,* CVIII (March 1, 1943), 292-93. On *Brownstone Eclogues.*

SHULENBERGER, ARVID. "From Senlin to Kilroy," *Poetry,* LXXVI (June, 1950), 162-66. Some interesting notes on New England heritage.

STAUFFER, DONALD A. "Genesis, or the Poet as Maker," *Poets at Work* (New York: Harcourt, Brace, 1948), pp. 37-82. Pp. 72-76, on Aiken's "Sursum Corda." An excellent MS study.

SYMONS, JULIAN. "The Poetry of Conrad Aiken," *Wake,* XI (1952), 107-13. A BBC broadcast.

TATE, ALLEN. "The Author of John Deth," *New Republic,* LXVIII (July 22, 1931), 265-66. Admires Aiken's talent, but regrets his waste of it.

WELLS, HENRY W. *New Poets from Old* (New York, 1940), pp. 291-306. Source study.

WINTERS, YVOR. Review of *Selected Poems, Hound and Horn,* III (April-June, 1930), 454-61.

Index